Ac

M.H. Bowker's rich, refreshing, and sometimes startlingly personal work is an intellectual-spiritual foray into the void at the center of our missing experience of being actually interested in our lives. It reminds us how often we seek and accept false substitutes for deep thinking and for truly coming alive. But it also guides us in coping with tedious academic pretense, with groupthink, with the artifices we layer over conflictual desires. Through his elegant, graceful, amusing, genuine, and welcoming writing, Bowker opens us to encounters with surprise, novelty, and provocation without cynicism. His singularity of voice and rarity of perception are reminiscent of the simultaneously trance-inducing and startling first-time effects of Winnicott, Bion, and Phillips. You will emerge from *Misinterest* awakened and with renewed focus and intentionality, as if from the best kind of guided meditation.

— Jill Gentile, author of *Feminine Law: Freud, Free Speech, and the Voice of Desire*

Psychoanalysis is a psychology of absences, a mode of thinking about the significance of what's missing. M.H. Bowker makes use of this psychoanalytic heuristic in his wonderfully provocative *Misinterest*. The book combines poetic, expository, and aphoristic forms, inviting readers into his stream-of-consciousness meditation on modern states of ennui. The essay "Is Sex Interesting?" is alone worth the read.

— Janice Haaken, Professor Emeritus of Psychology, Portland State University

Misinterest is a meditation on how we choose (Do we choose?) to pay attention; that is, to engage, or not to. Written with a Zen-like quality, I sometimes found myself wondering just what kind of volume was I reading — perhaps another mode of misinterest. Dr. Bowker's volume reads as part poem, part koan, part psychoanalytic free association. An indeterminate journey halfway between a documentary and a dream-book, I found *Misinterest* impossible to ignore.

— Dan Livney, Clinical Psychologist

MISINTEREST

Before you start to read this book, take this moment to think about making a donation to punctum books, an independent non-profit press,

@ https://punctumbooks.com/support/

If you're reading the e-book, you can click on the image below to go directly to our donations site. Any amount, no matter the size, is appreciated and will help us to keep our ship of fools afloat. Contributions from dedicated readers will also help us to keep our commons open and to cultivate new work that can't find a welcoming port elsewhere. Our adventure is not possible without your support.

Vive la Open Access.

Fig. 1. Hieronymus Bosch, *Ship of Fools* (1490–1500)

First published in 2019 by dead letter office, BABEL Working Group, an imprint of punctum books, Earth, Milky Way.
https://punctumbooks.com

The BABEL Working Group is a collective and desiring-assemblage of scholar–gypsies with no leaders or followers, no top and no bottom, and only a middle. BABEL roams and stalks the ruins of the post-historical university as a multiplicity, a pack, looking for other roaming packs with which to cohabit and build temporary shelters for intellectual vagabonds. We also take in strays.

ISBN-13: 978-1-950192-29-8 (print)
ISBN-13: 978-1-950192-30-4 (ePDF)

DOI: 10.21983/P3.0256.1.00

LCCN: 2019943080
Library of Congress Cataloging Data is available from the Library of Congress

Book design: Vincent W.J. van Gerven Oei

HIC SVNT MONSTRA

MISINTEREST

Essays, Pensées, and Dreams

by M.H. Bowker

Contents

Acknowledgments

I am deeply indebted to Eileen Joy for years of interest, inspiration, generosity, and support. This project, like so many others, would have been impossible — perhaps inconceivable — without her. I am obliged to Vincent W.J. van Gerven Oei for his immensely thoughtful editorial work and beautiful cover design.

I am grateful to David Levine, Fred Alford, Christian Hite, and Eduardo Frajman for their thoughtful comments on an early version of the essay, "Is Sex Interesting?" I have sought to address each of their concerns — some of which were, frankly, quite tough — in my revisions, but have not done so in ways in that would ultimately appease these generous friends and colleagues, who should not be considered to have endorsed the final product.

A portion of the essay "How to be a Victim: Camus's Plagues and Poisons" has been modified from a portion of *Ideologies of Experience: Trauma, Failure, Deprivation, and the Abandonment of the Self* (Chapter 6) published by Routledge in 2016.

A version of the essay "Civilizing Ironies" was published under a different title in *Clio's Psyche* 21, no. 3 (2014): 264–68.

For Zoe and Julie

What Is Missing

I.

A forgotten dream has an exquisite (*ex* + *quaerere*: sought out) quality.

That it is missed, and known to be missed—which is to say that we remember we've forgotten it—gives it a precious feeling, the timbre of a cloud.

The dream, itself, may be profound or banal: a revelation of a sacred truth or a nightmare about forgetting to wear shoes.

Someone will say a forgotten dream must be forgotten, is meant to be missed, as if we could know what is not meant to be known.

When we forget a dream, we miss a chance to hear a fragment of our wish and fear. In this sense, we miss a chance to be completely.

It is fair to ask, "Who can blame us for forgetting?"

It is fair to ask, "What if there were no dream?"

It is fair to ask, "What if the dream were not forgotten but imagined in order to be imagined to be forgotten?"

It is fair to dream about an ancient being who shared one's dream but did not forget.

The missing content of the forgotten dream may be the exquisite, itself, in its purest form: the unredeemable.

Still, it is unjust to consecrate such missing as meant to be.

To make missing meant to be is to say we're meant to miss being.

2.

When we call for an answer but hear no reply, we are tempted to mistake silence for missing and missing for mystery.

Investigations into mysteries are ill-fated because mysteries are made of things we determine to be meant to be missed.

Indeed, mysteries require silences, mute and magnify them, insisting that inconceivable words, prayers, or songs may be heard, but only if they are never articulated.

We make mysteries on behalf of our misinterest: a neologism (I know) needed to describe antipathy to interest.

Misinterest is, admittedly, a paradoxical concept, for we are not supposed to be averse to that which interests us, much less to interest, itself.

And yet misinterest is everywhere, compelling us to mistake, mishear, misunderstand.

Misinterest protects us from the grief of re(-)called misses, but does so at the cost of interest in life.

Why?

Because of the feeling: "not good enough."

If we are not good enough, we are not good enough to be.

Interest is a way of being; indeed, the heart of it.

Thus, guilt attends interest if we believe — even unconsciously — that we're unworthy of interest, missing what is needed, undeserving of being.

Efforts *not to be* occasion guilt as well, since most of us know — even unconsciously — that we need to be.

3.

If a parent were, for any reason, incapable of loving a child, that parent would do well enough to show the child interest.

For love is only interest of a very special sort.

Someone will object that love is infinitely more, that interest alone is not enough.

This objection, too, is made of misinterest, misused to serve love's mystery.

Very often one person loves another, even profoundly, even ferociously, but cannot hold love's central interest. Hence, love goes missing and becomes a mystery.

The making of missing love into a mystery is a tragedy with which any thoughtful person is familiar: familiar, in part, because it is, principally, familial.

4.

To the dilemma implied by this condition, a solution presents itself: to survive.

To survive is to be barely, to transpose the feeling, "not good enough to be," into the conviction, "To be barely is good enough."

Those who would be barely require deprivations, *environs* that recapitulate abandonments in which another was not good enough, but wherein thinking so would have been tantamount to death.

In such cases, to be "not good enough" is a means of surviving.

One cannot be barely amidst plenty. But the deprivations and abandonments referred to here are not concrete.

Instead, visible, tangible, audible surpluses of all sorts may surround the barely being beings who, nonetheless, have "not enough" at their centers.

5.

It is fair to ask whether we occupy ourselves with such investigations (*recherches, Forschungen*) to discover what we miss or to avoid it, whether we pursue *"la magique étude du Bonheur"* ["the magical study of happiness"] of which Rimbaud wrote wryly because it is a study *"que nul n'élude"* ["that no one escapes"] (1886), or in spite of its putative inevitability.

It is uncertain whether we may ask why we miss what is missing without indulging in a fascination with loss, whether we can truly perpendiculate the peripheries to which we are drawn, whether we can hold on to what is central, even as centrifugal forces seem to pitch us away.

Some find it distressing to discover that there is no such thing as "centrifugal force." Even what we feel to be "centrifugal" is a fiction born of an inertial frame, a frame we keep forgetting, like a dream, as we move and move, all the time missing what makes physical forces real: objects acting upon objects.

A Dream of Fundamentalist Resorts

I've made a terrible mistake and have driven my family to one of New York State's many Fundamentalist Resorts: resorts where Fundamentalists go to relax.

Needless to say, only Fundamentalists are permitted to enter.

The resorts are embassies of extremism, sovereign territories of Leisure and Law.

Those who attend them are more Fundamental than any creed. There is no question of doctrine. There are no Christians or Muslims or Jews: only Fundamentalists whose Fundamentalism surpasses all others'.

The Fundamentalists speak a language foreign to me, even though I speak all languages.

As we exit the car, four tremendous guards hurl themselves on me. My wife and daughter are torn from my side.

I am examined, inspected, interrogated.

The guards search my bags for items that would prove my piety, asking — now in English —about my toiletries.

Indeed, they are obsessed with my toiletries' insufficiency.

"These toiletries are for you!" they shout, between scoffs and curses.

I feel a pang of shame as I look at the items they've laid out on the bed.

"Why do I need such things just to—?"

"*Where!*" they interrupt my thought, "*Where* are the toiletries for God?"

At my despair, which they misinterpret as confusion, they kneel and mime a ritual of ablution—one performed a thousand times each day—with wide eyes and gaping mouths, drawing my attention to the cleaning of the face and ears.

I understand their question and their enactment, but I have no answer.

I have no toiletries for God, nor to cleanse myself to appear before God.

"I just take showers," I think. "And use Q-tips."

My family will be spared, but I will be killed.

Everyone knows I am not Fundamental.

I know it myself.

The question is how I have allowed myself to trespass into a Fundamental domain.

I begin to believe that I deserve my punishment.

In this moment, I sense that I am, at heart, a Fundamentalist.

But it is too late.

As I am hoisted up and carried away like Jesus, I hear the sounds of gentle fountains, children laughing, and people splashing in the Resort's clear, immaculate pools.

Poésie Banlieue, or, the Plano Suicides

1.

In the suburbs, gods are satisfactions.
Needs, therefore, blaspheme.
Unmet needs convert to *ectomies,*
which are insatiable and can only be filled up.
Some parents fill up their *ectomies* with children,
who are given unto suburban gods.

2.

Our *environs* were pretty pitches.
Yet suburbs are places superior to which we ought to be.
Mornings we had soft-boiled eggs in scarry mugs:
little, white, plastic things like outdoor teacups
or something someone else would throw away.
It's not like we refused.
There was nothing to which we were superior.

3.

Sliding patio doors rattled potted plants and wooden tables
whereupon soft-boiled eggs were served.
Streaky windows splintered sunlight on cat fur

and discolored spots of carpet,
on linoleum floors that smelled vaguely of pine.
You see, *environs* fill up *ectomies.*
Which is to say we lived in pitches
— pretty, scarry —
that became us.

4.

Suburbs such as ours produced people who would, later, become devoted listeners of Rush Limbaugh (2012a; 2012b), who dropped out of a suburban college and taught himself to say the terrible, sarcastic things the protolimbaughlisteners only thought:

> When you've taken more than your share and then you use that to flee the city, well, then you are held in contempt. And you have to be gotten even with [...]. The suburbs stole the wealth of the inner city [...]. In suburbia, that's where the good schools are. That's where the clean malls are [...]. Remember, the rich are to blame for everything. The achievers, those who succeed on their own, they are the ones to blame for all of these problems. You fled the inner cities when they needed you most. You took your money and you took your life and you took everything to the suburbs, and you left those who couldn't afford to go with nothing.

We knew who they were: children proud and angry, safe and dangerous.

No matter what we thought of the protolimbaughlisteners, we believed they loved themselves because their mothers loved them passionately.

(We were not politically correct and did not think of fathers because, frankly, in the suburbs of the 1970s and 1980s, mothers did most of the loving, or were supposed to.)

It was impossible not to be jealous of the mothers' love that, we thought, surely warmed, like sunlit windows unbesmirched by streaks, the tidy houses of the protolimbaughlisteners, a love that permitted its conferrees to experience their every wretched impulse as a kind of poetry.

We may not have stolen money or abandoned anyone, but our neighborhoods were, indeed, built on theft and segregation.

5.

At first, we rode bikes in stripmall parking lots. We smoked stolen low-tar cigarettes behind back-yard fences. We played in drainage pipes and dry, dirt fields. We loaded poorly hidden handguns. We got beaten up by parents and big brothers and football coaches and Deans of Discipline. We woke our teachers when they fell asleep at their desks.

In 1983 and 1984, a lot of us killed ourselves.

Again, in 1999, a lot more of us: half deliberately, half only half-deliberately, from heroin.

First, they called our deaths *clusters,* as in bombs or granola.

Then, they called them *waves,* as in tidal or "of grain."

Everyone feigned paroxysmal wordlessness and hid unwanted metaphorical boners.

Plano, Texas became "the suicide capital of the United States" (Block 2011; Durington 2008).

People loved that we amateurly shot average-quality dope and asphyxiated ourselves in pre-owned cars in attached garages.

These undesirable surprises validated surprising American desires: that a middling teenaged anybody could have a decent home of eggs and sunlight, play in the varsity game, hook up with a *Chili's* hostess, and then snuff himself right out.

"I think what parents in this situation find offensive," said a Dallas psychologist who requested not to be named, "is that by killing themselves, their sons and daughters are committing an ultimate act of rejection."

"The parents have worked to build what they consider the perfect lifestyle, and their children are saying [...] 'This lifestyle is so painful that I'd rather die.'" (Stiteler 1983).

Astonishing how much is missed in this statement.

6.

Banlieue is the French word for suburb.

It is a better word because a *banlieue* extends the *ban,* the jurisdiction of a city.

But *ban* also means the enforcement of the boundary: in and out.

Suburbs (*banlieues*) are not just places, but states of being wherein people find comfort at the perimeters of life, activity, interest.

The *lieue* in banlieue has nothing to do with a *lieu* (place)

Lieue is a unit of measure, like a "league," as in "twenty-thousand under."

Those who inhabit *banlieues* are not always comfortable. The physical comforts of the manifest suburbs attest to the psychic discomforts of metaphorical *banlieues.*

A *banlieue* is, by definition, what is not a center. The center is the thing to which a *banlieue* attends and upon which the *banlieue* depends. The center is that which the *banlieue* admires, but also that which the *banlieue* rejects.

A *banlieue* is banal and a place of abandonment [*abandonner*: from *mettre à bandon*].

Do suburbanites abandon their centers or have *banlieusards* been abandoned by what is — or what was once — central? Or are these two abandonments identical?

In any case, *banlieusards* remain bound to the very center from which they are banished.

Without tremendous effort, once *banlieusards,* we become inferior to the central life, thereafter circumnavigated with love and hatred, jealously and fear.

Most of us take our inability to escape our *environs* as evidence that we're unqualified for the central life, a life lived in and from our centers.

Most of us dedicate ourselves to re-creating and re-creating the manifest comforts and internal discomforts we know.

7.

Once, I walked into a suburban Methodist church on a weekday afternoon.

No parishioners were there, but some workers talked loudly in back.

An authoritative woman peered in, scowled at me.

She thought I was doing the talking.

The next time she passed by, I did everything in my power to appear silent, even though I was silent.

There is nothing we can do to appear more silent than we are.

Rather, there is only one thing we can do to appear more silent than we are.

A Dream of Psychoanalysis

I enter a "Holistic Center" for the first time and an analyst named Gary who wears large, round glasses informs me that he has prepared an "area" for me.

The area is furnished with small desks and daybeds that resemble prison cots.

Three or four men and women are already there, looking comfortable.

I am asked to sit on the mat in the center of the area.

I am content because, having been concerned about being unable to hear properly, I feel assured that from this position I will hear and be heard clearly.

Moreover, I feel confident that the terrible child with one, single, extraordinary eyebrow, who is always cutting in and out of my telephone calls from some location I shall never discover, will not be able to interfere.

Gary says, "I can assure you that what you will face here is a very different kind of enemy."

I sense immediately that Gary is knowledgeable about my enemy and about what I will face.

The session begins with a question about a yarn bracelet I am wearing.

I respond in lies and half-truths, stories about the bracelet's origin and meaning I've repeated so often I cannot remember, myself, whether they are false or true.

After I finish speaking, perhaps because I am lying, Gary ceases to pay attention to me.

The others in the area either have departed or have been extinguished from my consciousness.

I am suddenly aware that I can hear, through the thin walls, three or four other sessions going on at the same time.

I complain about this lack of confidentiality.

Gary mumbles something about "research purposes."

I then notice the playing of psychedelic music, as if it were being piped in through a set of invisible speakers.

I complain again, this time about the invasive music, to which Gary responds by pacing around the area.

But Gary does not remain in the area.

Rather, he conducts personal errands that are both inside and outside the area:

He remains with me but also goes to the ATM.

He gets gas.

He buys fast food.

He paces.

I wonder, "Is all of this part of the analysis?"

I ask Gary, "Can you tell me when we began, so I know when the session will be over?"

Gary tells me the incorrect time.

I know he has told me the incorrect time, so I ask again.

Now Gary is enraged and flips me off angrily, with both hands, while tucking himself into a small cubicle made of white foam-board.

I have had enough.

I scream, "Fuck you!" and "Fuck this!" and begin to feel very sorry for myself, which is a pleasurable, even ecstatic, feeling, as if I were finally able to register that a hurtful thing was happening to me.

In spite of this pleasure, or because of it, I try to leave the "Holistic Center," but am held back by several enormous attendants, who mock my complaint about being flipped off, as if it were my fault, as if I had misunderstood the meaning of the gesture.

They shout, "You are missing the boat, you fat fuck!"

I am, at this moment, primarily upset that these fat men think I am fat.

But I am also lucid enough to realize — now without the pleasure — that I am being abused.

The problem is that I have no idea how to act in relation to this abuse.

That is, I do not know how to avoid giving the abusers the satisfaction of proving me to be stupid, wrong, or weak, without, at the same time, giving up my own true hope that the abuse is good for me, which is identical to the wish that my abusers and my abuse will offer me answers, comforts, and other crucial things I need, which, of course, can only be delivered if I submit myself to "the process."

Audits *Maudits*

1.

Audits aren't all bad, although they seem so.

They're *hearings,* from the Latin, *audire.*

The most familiar, the tax audit, is generally unwelcome and, for some, a violent intrusion.

Even in its simplest sense, *to be heard* is ambivalent because, when heard, we may be misunderstood. On the other hand, when heard, we may be understood.

To understand means to "stand amidst," and so to occupy a place to hear. In Old English, *undersecan* meant to audit or examine. Even the Old High German root of *verstehen* means to "stand before," as if to hear or be heard directly.

Mishearing and misunderstanding are the bulk of the tragic and the comic: Euripides, Shakespeare, et cetera. But they are incomplete without the understanding that reveals them to miss the mark.

To hear the words that make us understand — or that make us understood, which may be the same — can be a blessing or a curse, can feel as if we've finally achieved our end, or can reveal that we've been played as fools all along, cast in an involuntary *audition,* danced upon a string.

When Oedipus finally hears the truth — a truth said, in its way, a dozen times, repeated silently inside him dozens more—he hears not merely the messenger's voice, nor the herdsman's, nor Tiresias's, nor the Oracle's, but, finally, his own. And when he does, he understands that he is the unwanted child, the curse upon his home.

In the wake of this epitomic audit *maudit,* it is a testament to Sophocles that Oedipus self-enucleates—puts out his eyes—instead of cutting off his ears—auriculectomy—condemning himself to hear and hear.

2.

Audit means *audience,* too. The audience is everyone, you and me, for we are audience to each other and to ourselves, as we think or read or write or speak.

Roland Barthes (1971) would say the audience is the author's collaborator, co-creating what is written or said. Better to say the author is the audience's co-auditor: hearing *with.*

It is fine to be an author, of a text or of a life, but it is terrible if we are not, at the same time, an audience, if we cannot hear ourselves.

Like the virtuoso who rehearses until she no longer hears the notes, we play most urgently to our internal audiences. Even our Rachmaninoffs or Bachs, our mothers, fathers, or Gods, are not invited.

In Tom Stoppard's *Rosencrantz and Guildenstern Are Dead,* the Player (travelling actor) knows, or fears, that without an audience, "by this time tomorrow we might have forgotten everything we ever knew" (1968, 22).

The real tragedy of these tragedians is that they lack the capacity to create an audience for themselves and are, therefore, enslaved to passers-by.

Their impotence of audience, if you will, is akin to dire loss, even trauma, perhaps death, itself.

Thus, the Player tells Rosencrantz and Guildenstern the effect of their abandonment:

> There we are — demented children mincing about in clothes that no one ever wore, speaking as no man ever spoke, swearing love in wigs and rhymed couplets, killing each other with wooden swords, hollow protestations of faith hurled after empty promises of vengeance — and every gesture, every pose, vanishing into the thin unpopulated air... Think, in your head, now, think of the most... *private... secret... intimate...* thing you have ever done secure in the knowledge of its privacy... Are you thinking of it? Well, I saw you do it! [...] No one came forward. No one shouted at us. The silence was unbreakable, it imposed itself upon us; it was obscene. (63–64, emphasis in original)

Not to have an audience when needed is as obscene and violent as to find an unwanted auditor investigating our secret, private selves.

There are within us tiny "incommunicado" nuclei that never speak to others (Winnicott 1965, 187), but their subtle languages may be heard by inner audiences if those audiences are exquisitely understanding.

Without such inner audiences, these centers are forever silenced, and with them, our capacity to hear, and to be.

3.

Maudit [pronounced: *mō-dē*] is French for cursed, from *mal* + *dire*: to speak ill.

It may be used casually, like its English equivalent: *"C'est un maudit bon biscuit!"* ["This is a damned good cookie!"].

But, more seriously, it is a swear: *"Cet audit maudit, c'est un cauchemar!"* ["This damned audit is a nightmare!"].

Although he didn't coin it, the phrase, *"poètes maudits"* [accursed poets] was made famous by Paul Verlaine, ordaining an unholy order of suffering artists. Verlaine's *Les poètes maudits* (1884) celebrated his exalted, abjected group.

Of course, Verlaine did not fail to include himself under the anagrammatic pseudonym, Pauvre Lélian (*Poor* Lélian), although he was thinking particularly of the curse of his young lover, Arthur Rimbaud, whom he shot with a revolver likely intended for himself.

Imagine, if you will, the auction cry when this weapon, drenched in pathos, sold for half a million Euros last year.

Isabelle de Conihout, perhaps speaking for *Christie's* (2016), called it "one of the most beautiful literary objects in existence."

Sometimes one hears things like this and thinks: "*Maudit soit le monde*" ["Fuck the world"].

Jeremiah (48:10) writes: "*Maudit soit celui qui fait avec négligence l'œuvre de l'Éternel*" ["Cursed is he who negligently does the work of the Eternal"].

But the real curse falls upon those who are neglected [*négligés*] by *l'Éternel,* who are never called to the central life, who never hear in their names reverberations of eternal interest.

That likely sounds bourgeois, as there are millions plagued by deadly afflictions, living in destitution, violated in unthinkable ways, tortured by genocide or war.

These are extremities of suffering, to be sure, but what makes them truly terrible is that they tend to lead the sufferers to lose interest in life, which is to say, to lose interest in being alive.

It is not to trivialize such horrors to remark that such loss is a fate worse than the death of the body.

"[Thomas] Hobbes was wrong when he said people fear their own violent death most of all," as Fred Alford gleaned from testimonies of Holocaust survivors (2009, 90). "Worse is the fear that the entire world has been emptied of value, all human attachment, Eros in its largest sense; in this impoverished world, only one's body remains."

4.

The loss of interest in life is not a mishearing or misunderstanding. Nor is it a mistake, although we are often mistaken in thinking that we are interested in our lives when, in fact, we are not.

The possibility of finding interest in life requires that we have developed the capacity to hear our central selves.

Likewise, if our children are to discover interest in their lives, then in their names they must hear our interest.

In their infantile cries and, later, in their adolescent and adult discourses, they must hear us hearing them.

Many people are incapable of hearing others because they cannot hear themselves. This holds not only for those for whom the task of hearing has been made infinitely harder by extraordinary grief or trauma.

It is the lucky, the gifted, the blessed among us who have been heard and who can hear: *les (bénits) entendus.*

5.

If we travel, we find not only an abundance of explicit suffering, but a profusion of persons for whom life holds no interest.

Not only have they no external audience, they lack internal audiences to attend the performances of their days. This is a simple truth we do not wish to hear.

We'd circle the Earth to avoid it, and, in doing so, find countless charming people who are fascinating *to us,* which is, of course, an utterly different matter.

To discover the truth about the *vie maudite,* we need only walk down a street long enough to find that area without interest, where it would appear as if a terrible machine had shorn from everything its vital vibrancy.

These areas may be middle-class suburbs or poverty-wracked regions, wealthy city blocks or trailer parks, Rust Belt townships or gated communities, not to mention the uncategorizable places no one knows how to name, like the lonely farmsteads along thoroughfares, or the neglected neighborhoods surrounding colleges and universities.

And that is just America. To go to Mexico, China, England, Indonesia, Cameroon, and walk down a street long enough is to see the same.

6.

Franz Kafka may be the great modern psychologist of audits *maudits* and misinterest, for he permits them — without naming them as such — to hold the ambivalence they deserve.

In "A Hunger Artist," the eponymous performer starves himself for a living. He comes to be dissatisfied with his art, just as his audiences lose interest in "the art of fasting."

But the artist is unhappy for reasons more complex than the public's. The artist is dissatisfied because he does not wish to hear the truth about himself, a truth that only he can hear: that his art is no art for him, although he wishes that it were.

His intimations of his fraud are expressed in his frustration projected upon his manager for setting limits to the duration of his fasts, not out of concern for the artist's health but because "after [about forty days] the town began to lose interest" (1971, 271).

It further annoys the artist that auditors of sorts are assigned to verify that he is not eating in secret at night, for the artist "would never in any circumstances, not even under forcible compulsion, swallow the smallest morsel of food; the honor of his profession forbade it" (268–69).

Even worse are advertisements such as "photographs [...] showing the artist on the fortieth day of a fast lying in bed almost dead from exhaustion. [...] What was a consequence of the premature ending of his fast was here presented as the cause of it! To fight against this lack of understanding, against a whole world of nonunderstanding, was impossible" (272–73).

In the end, the artist's performances cease to attract audiences, and he is hired by a circus and stationed at the periphery, along an entrance-route to the main attraction: a mere *amuse bouche* to the eventual *entrée.*

Neglected, his exhibition falls into disuse, the placard describing his performance becomes illegible, and the notice board counting the days of his fast is untouched for weeks or months.

So, the artist fasts amidst indifference and uncertainty: Even he loses track of the duration of his final fast, and although he is sure he's broken every record, he has no proof and no reward. He begins to die.

One day, the circus overseer and attendants pass by what they take to be an empty cage, for the hunger artist is so camouflaged by carelessness, as it were, that he barely *is* — which, it should be recalled, may well be the artist's true aim.

They poke around the cage with a stick, find the artist, and ask, "Are you still fasting?" and "When on earth do you mean to stop?"

To this the hunger artist asks for forgiveness and explains: "I always wanted you to admire my fasting [... b]ut you shouldn't admire it."

When asked why they shouldn't, the artist explains: "Because I have to fast, I can't help it."

"Why can't you help it?", they wonder, bemused.

And the artist whispers: "Because I couldn't find the food I liked. If I had found it, believe me, I should have made no fuss and stuffed myself like you or anyone else" (276–77).

We may speculate that the artist was never able to find the food he liked because he was never able to hear the call of his own hunger, his own desire, and instead, only the desire to be a center of attention for others, to nourish them by refusing to nourish himself, and so, to (ful)fill himself only by proxy.

What the hunger artist finally admits is that he does not fast at all, that his art is a charade, that he is merely averse to food, that he is, therefore, nothing special, just a man who eats or does not eat according to his preference, like everybody else.

That he "feeds" on attention rather than on food destroys the possibility of interest in his performances, presented as exercises in superhuman self-control, but, in fact, displays of self-mishearing, loss of appetite, and being barely.

Perhaps modern audiences are on to him. More likely, modern audiences are, themselves, so near to being barely that they do not wish to see it enacted before them on a stage.

Perhaps they'd rather avoid the thought of it altogether, finding distraction in something, anything else, even that which is uninteresting, so long as it is lively, such as the panther that takes over the artist's cage.

The panther eats huge chunks of meat with a "joy of life" that "streamed with such ardent passion from his throat that for the onlookers it was not easy to stand the shock of it. But they braced themselves, crowded around the cage, and did not ever want to move away" (277).

7.

In a parable related to "A Hunger Artist," Kafka describes "the most insatiable people," such as Kafka himself, as "certain ascetics, who go on hunger-strike in all spheres of life" (1971, 488–89).

They hope that in doing so they will hear a voice — a polyphony, really — say all of the following at once:

1. You have fasted enough to become special. Now, you may eat like others but "it will not be accounted unto you as eating."
2. Your fasting will no longer be difficult for you. "You will now fast with joy, it will be sweeter than food (at the same time, however, you will also really eat)."
3. "You have conquered the world, I release you from it." And you will now both eat and not eat.
4. "Though you do not fast completely, you have the good will, and that suffices."

These are the words a child longs to hear.

As bizarre as they are, these words carry the central meanings that must be audible within the self, if the self is to hear anything else of value.

A Dream of Not Swinging

I am at a swingers' party with my wife.

I do not like it at all.

The other couples are starting to pressure us to do things.

But before anything can be done, we must write the word "sex" on a piece of paper and put it in a bowl.

This ritual has something to do with "consent."

I know I will never write it.

When asked about my resistance, I say, to my own surprise, that I feel the way I felt when I lost hope in Austin, Texas.

For several months, I tell the crowd — whose attention turns to me without any effort of my own — I chased a feeling of obliteration, even of death, because — I struggle to find the words — I wanted to meet it, because I sought a kinship, because I wished to die, or at least would have preferred to die than to go on living as I was.

At this honest admission, I begin to weep and am surprised by my emotions.

Concerned about the group's response, I am surprised — now for a third time — by the crowd's immediate and unconditional supportiveness.

Sarah Palin helps me sit down in a soft chair.

I remain committed to my refusal to partake in swinger sex and am ready to leave, but am paralyzed by overwhelming feelings of guilt.

I cannot move from my chair because I am so concerned that I have disappointed the group.

I am convinced that I have ruined their swingers' night, that the story I told was a turn-off, that I have abused the group in ways more thoughtless, more odious than those in which I feared they would abuse my wife and me.

Is Sex Interesting?

1.

Ten years ago, Wallace Shawn wrote an essay called, "Writing About Sex" (2009), reprinted in *Harper's Magazine* under the title, "Is Sex Interesting?"

I have revived — a euphemism for *copied* — this title in large part because Shawn's essay neither asks nor answers the titular question.

Part of me wonders if the misleading title was suggested not by Shawn but by an enterprising *Harper's* editor who, while failing to grasp Shawn's piece, nevertheless succeeded in formulating an intriguing question.

2.

Is sex interesting?

I would like to address the matter as fair-mindedly as possible.

To that end, I confess that my instinct is to say: "Obviously, sex is *not* interesting."

I assume there are others, perhaps a majority, whose instinctive responses are opposite.

The thing to do, of course, is to get away from intellectual instinct — a euphemism for *prejudice* — altogether, and to think the matter through.

While on the subject of instinct, however, it seems worthwhile to remark that our instincts, whether physical or intellectual, need not be interesting to hold force. That is, we do not engage in instinctual activities *because* they are interesting.

Of course, some people are uniquely drawn to activities with instinctual aspects — and, indeed, what human activity does not have some instinctual aspect? Nevertheless, they may be drawn to such activities with varying levels of what we might call instinctual engagement. Chefs or restaurant critics, for instance, who are interested in food do not approach food primarily as a matter of instinct, although their instinctive responses to smells, tastes, textures, and colors very likely inform their work.

Similarly, paleo-scatologists may or may not have instinctual attractions or aversions to feces, but, in either case, we may hope, their instinctual attractions or aversions do not enter into their scientific work.

It becomes a different matter if we consider not those who take studied approaches to subjects associated with activities with instinctual aspects or attributes, but those who are *preoccupied* with such activities beyond the degree implied by either study or instinct. In such cases, we speak not of scatological science, but of scatological fetish or coprophilia; not of gastronomy or culinary art, but of compulsive eating, food addiction, or anorexia.

Although human sexuality is considerably more complex than the phrase, "activities with instinctual aspects" suggests, most would agree that sex retains vital connections with instinct, which is merely one way of saying that, whatever we mean by "sex" — which is, of course no simple matter — we do not ignore the physiology of vasodilation, lubrication, ovulation, ejaculation, and so on.

To be sure, physiological phenomena are difficult if not impossible to separate from emotions and intellects, for even a touch may be more or less sexually arousing if it comes from someone who is loved, or if one judges it to be morally wrong. At the same time, it is possible to engage in sexual activities with which, either by design or by accident, our emotions and intellects are relatively uninvolved.

That interest is not the driver of instinct cannot be counted as evidence that instinctual activity is uninteresting. Nevertheless, it is reasonable to assert that instinctual activity — not the thought of it, nor the study of it, but the *doing* of it — is uninteresting *because* it is instinctive, unthought, and unconscious. Instinctual doing is boring, by definition.

3.

I have now introduced a distinction that would get me into trouble among colleagues who argue that distinguishing between doing and thinking entrenches a Cartesian, dualistic outlook. (What a boring objection this has become!)

To address the question of the interest of sex we must be able to acknowledge that it may be regarded in two ways: as a topic of possible intellectual interest and as an activity with which we may or may not be engaged, owing to any number of factors, one of which may well be our degree of interest in sex.

If we are so anti-Cartesian as to be unable to accept this premise, if we cannot imagine a way to distinguish, even roughly, between thinking and doing, then we are stuck, and we may wish to consider how and why we have become so stuck.

I submit that our stuckness on this point is, in fact, related to our opinions concerning the interest of sex, particularly the fantasy of fusion that informs our attitudes toward sex and sexuality.

The fantasy of fusion suggests that, in sex, bodies, persons, categories of experience, and even contradictory thoughts and feelings all collapse into each other, becoming one.

This fantasy, that sex overcomes difference (and *différance*), duality, subjectivity, sovereignty, individuality, and more, may be understood — and, for centuries, even for millennia, *has been* understood — as a counter-point to the outlook we now call

Cartesian: a vision of the world as consisting of separate persons, and a vision of persons as having minds that are to some degree distinguishable from bodies.

4.

Let us consider this matter in a different way. It is possible — although not necessary or obvious — to regard the basic bodily activities of eating, sleeping, sex, excretion, and all the others (digesting, breathing, blinking, coughing, and so on) as immensely boring, possibly as the most boring things in the world.

At the same time, when undertaken in interesting ways or with interesting people, at least some of these activities may become interesting.

If we can speak of the activity of dining and not the thought or study of it, we may suggest that, at least for most people, what is interesting about dining is not that food happens to be passing through their alimentary tracts, but that, if certain conditions are met, interesting sensations, including taste, emotions, experiences, contemplations, or imaginations may be had.

The meal, itself, may have been prepared thoughtfully, creatively, or with a sense of experimentation, and these qualities may also be appreciated by the diners.

In the same way, if we may speak about the doing of sex and not the thought or study of it, what is most interesting about sex is not that certain body parts, or extensions of body parts, are meeting other body parts, but that, if certain similar conditions are met, interesting sensations, emotions, experiences, contemplations, or imaginations may be had.

So, we see now why the question of "whether sex is interesting" is, in some important sense, too blunt to answer directly.

Sex may be interesting if we make sex interesting. To make sex interesting, we must remain capable of generating and of holding interest in sex while in the presence of the rudimentary *doing* of sex, as it were.

And to remain capable of this feat, we must discover and respect boundaries between ourselves, as interested persons, and the objects of our interest, just as we must respect the boundaries between ourselves, as interested persons, and the other persons with whom we are sexually engaged or in whom we are sexually interested.

5.

While it is common to say that doing a thing (throwing javelins or making music or playing chess) "is interesting," we typically mean that doing a thing sponsors interesting ideas, potentialities, imaginations, reflections, and so on. These we entertain primarily before or after the moments, or micro-moments, of immediate doing.

To borrow the (boringly) popular concept of "flow" from Mihaly Csikszentmihalyi (1990), it is awkward and likely inaccurate to say that athletes or musicians or chess players who are thoroughly engrossed in their activities are — while "in the zone" or "in the groove" or "in the moment of flow" — *interested* in javelins or French horns or the Sicilian defense. Rather, they are more and less than interested.

Even the most enthusiastic athlete, musician, or chess player must spend hours running laps, practicing scales, rehearsing matches, and so on. We all must find a way to appreciate, or at least to tolerate, the tedious aspects of what we do, if we are to thrive. But no matter what activity we are involved in, we cannot remain in a state of "peak" interest throughout the entirety of our lives. If we expect to, we are sure to be disappointed.

What is more, "peak" interest is not likely to be achieved in the same moment as "peak" performance. This is but one reason why we do not exclaim to our partners, or even to ourselves, during sex: *"How interesting this sex is!"*

Rather, "peak" interest requires "room" or "space" for interest, where imagination and creativity and reflection can enter into what we are doing. Sometimes, this requires a literal or figurative separation or "stepping back" from our doing, so that we can observe it, consider it, and appreciate it. Sometimes, it is possible to do and to find space to appreciate what we are doing simultaneously.

"But what makes sex interesting," someone will say, "is *precisely* that, in sex, we cease to be capable of stepping back and are locked in our doing. We cease to exist as bounded beings or separate persons or minds that can wander away and, instead, because of the intensity and immediacy of the activity, become identified with, enveloped by, intertwined with, enmeshed with sex and with those with whom we are sexually engaged."

This vision of sex as a kind of eclipse of the separate, thinking, potentially interested self I have referred to above as the sexual "fantasy of fusion." It is a fantasy not because it is impossible or unreal but because it is a *wished-for* experience that entails not only the wish for engrossing sexual encounters but the wish for the loss of the self and the wish to discover, even momentarily, that one is indistinguishable from another, that one is a part of something greater than one's self.

6.

Before anything else, we should remember that sex is *not unique* in its capacity to intertwine or enmesh persons, bodies, and/or objects, unless we are thinking of sex in a childishly literal sense.

There are innumerable events and activities that entangle people and so offer challenges — of varying degrees, of course — to their sense of separateness.

For better or for worse, our sense of separateness may be challenged, to a degree equal to if not greater than that invoked by sex — by telling a secret, making a home, speaking a terrible truth, sharing a terrible lie, discovering a partner, discovering one has cancer, giving birth to a child, raising a child, losing a child, and more.

On this point, D.W. Winnicott (1986) reminds us that Edward Albee's famous play, "Who's Afraid of Virginia Woolf," depicts two persons ensnared in a gruesome struggle over a child who *does not exist.* That is, the child has been conceived *only* in the imagination, not via sexual conception.

All sexually active adults have likely had at least one encounter in which they found their sexual activities to be—deliberately or accidentally—*decoupled* from their sexual partners. It would be quite surprising if most sexually active adults had not had at least one experience of doing a sexual thing in a way that bore little or no relation to the other person or persons with whom they were ostensibly sexually engaged.

In such instances, although our bodies may have been entwined in sexual activity, our thoughts and feelings and imaginations were in different worlds: Perhaps we were still annoyed by a nasty email from a colleague, or perhaps we feared we would wake up the baby, or perhaps we found ourselves imagining an entirely different sex act, or perhaps we found ourselves fantasizing about engaging with an entirely different sexual partner.

The fact that we may have, at one time or another, had sex in which we did not achieve the kind of subsumption or envelopment by another that is supposed to be sex's central virtue has not prevented us from continuing to believe that in sex lies a rebellion against and an escape from the separate self.

Thus, the more one considers the sexual fantasy of fusion, the more sex appears as but one of many avenues by which we experiment with the possibility of *not being,* i.e., not being ourselves, becoming less or more, or being something or someone else.

7.

It is awkward to say that a person holds an interest in *not being,* although it is undeniable that not being is a subject replete with both fascination and boredom.

If we can imagine persons interested in not being, then it would be well to know what part or parts of those persons hold this interest in not being.

The part of the person that *is not*?

The part of the person that is not truly alive, and so wishes that the rest of the person would *not be* along with it?

The part of the person that hates the person's being, and wishes only to be involved with doing, so that the person remains hidden, obscured, neglected, unto death?

The desire to lose oneself, to become something other than oneself, or simply not to be are expressions of a lack of interest in living, or, put only slightly differently, a lack of interest in living as oneself.

In this way, sexual activity and sexual fantasy are not rooted in interest, but in its opposite.

8.

After sharing drafts of this essay with several colleagues, those with expertise in what may be called "sex studies" took me to task for failing to engage with the theoretical and critical literatures on sex and sexuality, whereas I wished to focus on the question of the *interest* of sex, a subject about which very little has been written.

Their objections, I think, were rooted in the sense that I was being old-fashioned by not assenting to the contemporary belief discussed above: that the interest of sex inheres in its disruptive quality: that sex challenges subjectivity and the "fantasy of sovereignty" in some way or other (see Berlant & Edelman 2013).

It is true that I feel no need to discuss in detail ideas such as Jacques Lacan's famous insistence that "*Il n'y a pas de rapport sexuel*" (1970, 134). Like so many of Lacan's adages, this one may be and has been translated in a variety of ways, including:

"There is no sexual relation(ship)," and/or, "There is no sexual intercourse," and/or, "There is no relation between sexes," and/or, "There are no sexes."

In my view, in any permutation of meaning, this statement is more confusing and boring than enlightening and interesting.

The same may be said for Michel Foucault's well-known quip that "sex is boring" (2000, 253), which, while it would seem to cohere with my own thesis, I would argue to be best understood as a disingenuous attempt to be provocative, Foucault having devoted so much of his life and work to sex and sexuality.

As for the others — Reiss or Sedgwick or Dworkin — I dislike reading them. Yet mine is not a prudish aversion. I merely find it tiresome to read about sex, much in the same way I find it tedious to read about "the Anthropocene" or "neoliberalism" or "privilege" or, thirty years ago, "globalization."

Consider what is offered to those who wish to read about sex. On the very first pages of Alenka Zupančič's (2017) book, heralded by Jean Copjec as "an event" that "restores to sex its florid obscurity" — as if restoring something to obscurity were a good thing for a book to do! — we are told that the person who sublimates a sexual urge into, say, talking, does not obtain a substitute satisfaction of an inferior order. Rather, the person who talks achieves a satisfaction in talking that is "exactly the same" as the satisfaction of sex.

What is more, this satisfaction in talking is not only commensurate with that of sex, but "the satisfaction in talking is *itself* 'sexual'" (2017, 1, emphasis in original), because sex is "the operator of the inhuman" (7), which is actually a kind of confounding code-phrase for: "that which turns us into human subjects."

"Human sexuality," then, is "the point at which the impossibility (ontological negativity) pertaining to the sexual relation appears as such, 'registers' in reality as its part" (16).

Talking, playing the piano, writing, whistling, walking: All of these activities are "sexual," on this line of thought.

Human civilization, itself, is "sexual" because it is "a stand-in for something within the sexual which 'is not.'"

And even that which we cannot comprehend about our civilization we do not grasp or comprehend because these things, *too,* are sexual, for *"Il n'y a de sexe que de ce qui cloche"* ["In what goes wrong, there is only sex"] (23).

"When we come across something and have absolutely no clue what it is," Zupančič concludes, "we can be pretty certain that it 'has to do with sex'" (23).

Here — and not only here — sex becomes that which structures our reality and that which disrupts it.

Sex explains everything and underwrites the inexplicable.

Sex is the missing link or "short circuit" between ontology and epistemology.

Sex is the root of all knowledge and all confusion.

Sex is the mysterious essence of Being (see Zupančič, 2017, 141–42).

After reading such things about sex, I feel a bit as Rimbaud must have felt, in his torpor, with his loved and loathed Verlaine, writing (1886):

J'ai fait la magique étude
Du Bonheur que nul n'élude.

Roughly translated, this means: "I have completed the magical study of the Happiness no one escapes."

Or, translated to rhyme, and tortured a bit: "I have studied the magical shapes of the Happiness no one escapes" (Rimbaud 2000, 39).

Both translations obscure an important double meaning in the couplet: It is both the Happiness that no one escapes, *and* the study, the research (*recherche*) that no one escapes. It is to both that Rimbaud attributes a certain terrible inevitability, as if they were both forced labor.

There is suffering, for Rimbaud, in this study of happiness. The remainder of the poem tells us that it depletes Rimbaud's "*envie*" ["desire"], takes charge of Rimbaud's life, steals Rimbaud's "*âme et corps*" ["soul and body"], and dissipates "*tous efforts*" ["all Rimbaud's efforts"].

Why?

In an irony that Lacanians will understand but will not appreciate, virtually all writing about sex overloads the signifier ("sex") such that it, in turn, overwhelms any signifieds to which it might refer.

That is to say: "Sex" overwhelms the other signifiers to which it may be related, collapsing the fragile web of signification — meaning — in which we live.

I do not wish to delve deeply into semiotics here, but it should be clear that there is no question of treating "sex" as a signal or direct representation of a "raw object" or "real phenomenon."

"Sex" is a concept that, at best, refers us to other concepts in a signifying chain, never directly to a "thing-in-itself."

To understand this, alone, suggests that there may be limited value to quibbling over whether we are discussing the conceptual interest of sex or the interest of participating in sex acts. To be sure, we have concepts both for sexual activity and for thinking about sex, and these concepts are distinct. But the problem of the overwhelming signifier arises *before* this distinction has a chance to matter.

In spite of the pretense of understanding, or the pretense of wishing to understand, the nature and meaning of sex — the title of Zupančič's book is: *What Is Sex?* — those who write about sex often make sex less understandable, and I see no reason to assume that this result is accidental.

Often, those who write about sex break the *sign* that is "sex."

That is, they destroy the relation between the signifier ("sex") and the concept signified, seemingly in order to re-enact within their texts the fantasy that already underwrites them: that "sex" is a disruptive force.

The study (*recherche*) of sex is conducted, again and again, but the meaning of sex is broken, again and again, perhaps in order to make "sex" seem "raw," and "real," perhaps in order to preserve the fantasy of sex as the great prison-break, the escape from signification, meaning, being, and thought.

Needless to say, the result is a discourse about sex that succeeds in reifying (i.e., making concepts into things-in-themselves) "sex," but also makes "sex" utterly incomprehensible and profoundly boring.

9.

There is more than a little (semi-conscious, unconscious) aggression at work here. Making sex boring — allowing "misinter-

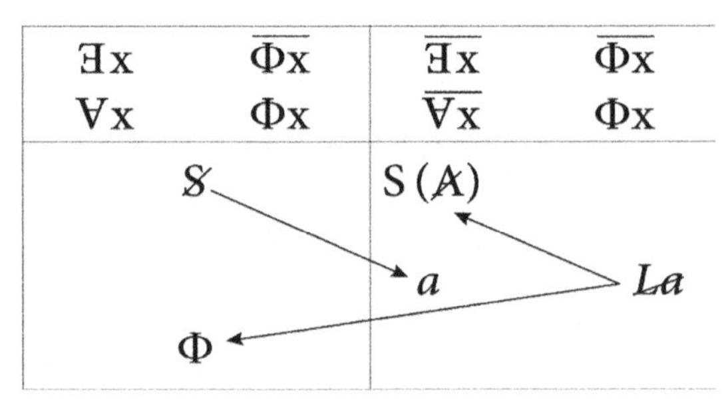

Figure 1. The diagram of sexual difference. © J. Lacan, CC BY 4.0.

est" to pervade the discourses of sex—is akin to a kind of mystification of sex, barring opportunities to make sex meaningful.

Consider the presentation of the following information (fig. 1) to an audience—even an audience of *initiates*—under the pretense of facilitating their understanding or interest (Lacan 1975, 73).

Lacan's famous description of sexuation and sexual difference—in which the left column refers to the "male" and the right, the "female"—presents one obvious (formal) logical contradiction—"Everyone is submitted to the phallic function," and "There exists someone who is not submitted to the phallic function."

This contradiction, then, is transformed into a source of mystery (see Boudry 2014), and, then, into the kind of fascination inspired by the suggestion of a knowledge that escapes thought.

Indeed, Lacan warns his audience: "After what I just put on the board, you may think you know everything. Don't" (1998, 78).

How could we?

Why is it important to chasten us for thinking as much?

And doesn't this act of chastening, itself, suggest that Lacan *does,* in fact, know everything, even or especially that which is unknowable?

If the ways in which we write about sex degrade or destroy our thinking about it, and, therefore, degrade or destroy any mature interest we may have in it, then, in spite of presumptions about sex's interest, they betray an impulse not to think about sex, not to understand sex, not to make sex meaningful, and, strangest of all, *not to make sex interesting.*

The despair and ennui of Rimbaud, although enjoying what was by all accounts a vibrant, yet also violent, romantic life with Verlaine, when considered in the light of our efforts to keep sex beyond our understanding, suggests that sex is perhaps best described as a subject of fascination *and* a subject of boredom *at the same time.*

The combination of fascination and boredom is an experience for which we do not have a word.

I have suggested the term "misinterest," although I am always hesitant to invent a new piece of jargon.

Whatever we choose to call it, this coincidence of fascination and boredom is not at all the same as *interest*. In fact, it is perhaps the closest thing we have to interest's opposite, working directly against it.

10.

Someone will say: "Few subjects in the history of human civilization have received as much attention as sex. Surely such sustained attention proves that sex is interesting."

First, we might benefit from considering the meaning of "interest" in relation to attention, a subject which, perhaps ironically, has not been of great interest to philosophers or psychologists.

William James understood interest to be the cause of attention: "The things to which we attend are said to interest is. Our interest in them is supposed to be the cause of our attending" (1950, 416).

And others have followed suit by defining interest as the "conative" quality of our attention (Berlyne 1949), which is about as helpful as saying, to cite the famous fallacy, that opium puts people to sleep because of its soporific properties.

John Dewey introduced a rather important psychological term into the question of the meaning of interest by suggesting that the aim of interest is the "identification" of the interested person with the object of interest (1913, 27), so that the person must be interested in it, lest she lose interest in her very self.

It is a revolting idea, especially if we recall that much of Dewey's work was intended to be used—and continues to be used—as a guide for inculcating interest in school-aged children and young adults for the advancement of politically and economically rewarding ends.

It is tempting to imagine that the psychological phenomenon we call "interest" is related to the moral and economic construct we call "self-interest"—because, presumably, when we take an interest, we see in interest's object something that holds the potential to enrich us.

But interest, in the psychic sense, is not an instrument. We are not interested instrumentally, in order to enrich ourselves.

Or, at least, it is not very helpful to use the term, "interest," to describe this kind of appropriative attention.

We may say, in a casual sense, that so-and-so is interested in earning money, but we rarely mean that this person finds money interesting.

Rather, paradoxically, the pursuit of interest is disinterested. And the destruction of psychic interest appeals (unconsciously) to our self-interest, even to our greed, from which real interest may be a distraction, or worse.

It may appear ironic that, in an age of capitalism and individualism, where our "attention" suffers "deficits" and where many are driven to distraction, we would seek to destroy interest.

Any irony here is merely apparent because, even if we envisage self-interest as "self-interest properly understood," it is well-known that individuals, groups, and societies frequently act in ways contrary to their own proper interests: We damage the environment, we make laws and support norms that impoverish us and make us unhappy, we repeat destructive patterns in behaving and relating.

Rather, to be interested in something is to open a channel of communication, to enter an *auditorium,* if you will, between persons and interesting objects, which may be ideas, other persons, things, et cetera. Self-interest guards against interest because interest implies an opening, a communication with something central in our selves.

The most important interest is interest in being, in living as oneself.

This interest requires an internal audience that both hears and is heard.

To develop this internal audience one must have been fortunate enough to have had external audiences to internalize, as well as a capacity to bear the possibility not only of being misunderstood but, what may feel even more terrifying, of being understood.

Those who lack these audiences and capacities avoid interest like the plague (see also *How To Be a Victim: Camus's Plagues and Poisons,* this volume).

II.

To return to the hypothetical objection raised earlier—that sustained historical attention to sex proves that sex is interesting—we might also reply by inquiring whether our perseverance in attending to sex really evinces its interest, or, rather, reflects, to borrow an ugly term from psychiatry, a *perseveration,* a preoccupation, a compulsion, an obsession, a fascination?

Is it not likely that our attention to sex—and there is no denying that we attend to it relentlessly—expresses not an interest rooted in the intellectual and emotional potentialities sex may hold for us, but, rather, a perseveration rooted in a fascination with compulsive, rote, and repetitive activity, i.e., a *boring* perseveration?

Let us consider what it means to "fascinated." As Gustave Le Bon describes it, the fascinated person has "entirely lost his conscious personality" and has become, instead, "an automaton who has ceased to be guided by his will."

"The state of 'fascination'" is the state "in which the hypnotized finds himself in the hands of the hypnotizer" (quoted in Freud 1959, 11).

If we are fascinated by sex, on this account, what draws us to sex is not interest but something far less intelligible, far less conscious.

The word "fascination" captures it well, being derived from the Latin *fascinare,* meaning to bewitch, enchant, even enslaved. Perhaps being bound to sex, in this sense, is what binds us to sex, in another sense. In any case, to be spell-bound is not to be interested.

Psychological ambivalence plays an important role in fascination, because that which fascinates us does so because we find ourselves enticed and repulsed.

We are rarely aware of our ambivalences, and we are often incapable of admitting them to ourselves or others.

Thus, it is not uncommon to mistake ambivalence for fascination, since we keep coming back to that about which we are most conflicted, as if returning to the scene of a crime we wish both to erase and to endlessly repeat.

Where there is ambivalence, there is hiding, or, to use the psychological term: *repression.* What we repress are the "valences" with which we are most uncomfortable. We acknowledge love in the family more readily than hate, revulsion at death more readily than revulsion at birth, the allure of sex more readily than the allure of violence.

Susan Sontag's (1975) review essay, "Fascinating Fascism," worries about the popularity of fascistic imagery. Despite the appearance suggested by her title, one has to go back quite a distance to find an etymological link between "fascism" and "fascination," beyond any modern language, beyond Latin and ancient Greek, and ultimately to the Proto-Indo-European root, *bhasko,* meaning something like a bundle or band or, perhaps, phallus (see Watkins 2000).

For Sontag, fascism sponsors fascination because we are fascinated by sadomasochistic sexuality, by "situations of control, submissive behavior [...] relations of domination and enslavement [...] the turning of people into things [... or] the orgiastic transactions between mighty forces and their puppets."

Of course, not all sex is sadomasochistic and thus, to allude to her essay here is not to imply that our long-standing fascination with sex can be accounted for by fascination with sadomasochistic sex. Rather, we may be fascinated both with fascism and with sex to the extent that part of us wishes to submit to the force of sex. If fascism can be, for lack of a better term, "sexy," it is also true that, even absent patent elements of sadomasochism, *sex can be fascistic.*

Think of Wallace Stevens's early poem "*Le Monocle de Mon Oncle,*" whose title, aside from being silly, alludes to the viewpoint of a more mature "uncle," or—if one considers vulgar slang terms for the phallus, such as "one-eyed snake"—an uncle's penis.

The most memorable stanza (XI) begins:

> If sex were all, then every trembling hand
> Could make us squeak, like dolls, the wished-for words. (1990, 17)

Thank goodness we are not wind-up dolls, squeaking out determined words, however wished-for those words may be.

Instead, the "unconscionable treachery of fate"—to be said with tongue in cheek—has both exiled (banned) us and liberated us from a half-Edenic, half-sexually-totalitarian state in which we resided in our youth. As we mature, we live, think, and act in other regions and on other registers, "without regard / To that first, foremost law" (17).

Early in Plato's *Republic,* Socrates and his friends meet Cephalus, a man who is "as the poets say, about to cross the threshold" into death (328e). Cephalus tells them that, unlike many of his elderly acquaintances who lament their waning libidos and the loss of their youthful enjoyments, he finds himself content. "In fact," he continues

> I was once present when someone was asking the poet Sophocles about sex, and whether he was still able to make love to a woman; to which he replied, "Don't talk about that;

> I am glad to have left it behind me and escaped from a fierce and frenzied master." A good reply I thought then, and still do. For in old age you become free of feelings of this sort and they leave you in peace, and when your desires lose their intensity and relax, you get what Sophocles was talking about, a release from a lot of mad masters.

This notion of sex as "mad" master, or as law, or as hypnotizer or puppeteer, suggests, of course, that, in sex, one may not be one's own master, that sex may take command and compel one to (boringly) comply.

To the extent that we entertain this fantasy about sex, in which we are disrupted by another, we may actually be identifying not with the vulnerable, open subjectivities we praise but with the mad master, the sovereign of sex, Sex *Rex,* as it were.

Whether we find this possibility sexually arousing or not, it remains true that, to the extent that we experience sex as ruler, law, or superior power, as something that subjugates or objectifies us, sex cannot really hold interest for us, as we are incapable of generating and holding onto our own interest while in a subjugated, objectified state.

12.

Consider the following possibilities, which cannot be proven, nor disproven:

Interest is impossible without understanding.

Without understanding, what might have been an object of interest can become only an object of fascination, or boredom, or both.

We become fascinated with that which we do not understand in part because we do not understand it.

We may begin by feeling dominated and even bored by that which we do not understand to the degree that it is opaque. It withholds from us, or seems to withhold from us, what is interesting in it.

And yet, this withholding frustrates and fascinates us.

We attribute to it a mysterious power.

The object that cannot be understood is a screen for our projections, a totem for occult worship.

To relate to this object is not to relate to the object, itself, but to that which imposes upon the object.

We can only be interested in that to which we can relate.

13.

Teaching a university class in which students and I encounter a text or film that contains sexual material can be an interesting or boring experience, depending in large part on the class's willingness to consider the possibility that sex is more or less than what it seems to be.

In many films, for example, sex is portrayed as both the evidence and apex of intimacy. It seems to me that sex is so prevalent in film mainly because sex is visually transmissible and titillating, whereas the complex emotions and qualities of relationship for which sex is sometimes but a crude metaphor — including not only intimacy, but desire, love, need, aggression, greed, and despair — are less so.

Likewise, class discussions about sex are interesting or boring depending upon the degree of stuckness the group evinces in thinking about such subjects, which may be understood in terms of at least two main sources of resistance: (1) resistance to the possibility that sex is understandable in terms that are not themselves sexual, and (2) (what amounts to the same thing) resistance to the idea that sex may be — but need not be — a physical expression of something more important than sex, such that films or texts that seem to be about sex may not be about sex at all.

"What could be more important than sex?" someone will ask, perhaps with a laugh.

"Eros," one might answer, which includes not just sex but interest in life, in the self and in others, love, attachment, meaningfulness, and vitality, all combined into one.

One can have Eros without having sex, and one can have sex without having Eros.

It seems important, in classrooms and elsewhere, to reflect on the possibility that sex may be used as a substitute for, distraction from, or denial of Eros.

14.

Someone will say, again perhaps with a laugh: "If you doubt that sex is interesting, you must be doing it wrong."

This hypothetical riposte — along the lines of Louis Armstrong's well-known claim that "if you have to ask what jazz is, you'll never know" — is both misguided and subtly aggressive.

It is misguided because no one would insist that someone who doubts the interest of jogging or watching soap operas must be incapable of performing either of those activities. Such a comment would not even elicit a smile or a laugh, just confusion.

It is aggressive because it is, essentially, a joke, and, as we might have learned from Freud (1960), jokes typically come at someone's expense. Jokes activate and release, in socially acceptable forms, aggressive impulses.

This particular joke neuters its target, implying that the person who doubts the interest of sex must be incompetent, flaccid, impotent, or sexually inadequate in some way.

In this case, I am the hypothetical target of my own hypothetical attack, so I use the gender-specific terms, "flaccid" and "impotent."

But the same joke could be applied, and *has been applied,* with considerably oppressive intent, to women who dared to question the interest of sex. In such cases, the joke-makers simply change the derogatory terms from "flaccid," for instance, to "frigid."

The joke turns the question of interest on its head, transforming what began as an inquiry into a threat: "If you are not interested in sex, then sex won't be interested in you."

So, when Armstrong says, "you'll never know," he exiles the targets of his joke, insisting that they shall never belong. He establishes a barrier and a ban around the group and casts out not necessarily jazz musicians or jazz critics or even jazz haters but anyone who would inquire about the definition of the activity that holds the group together.

What holds the group together is what, in psychoanalytic language, we call "the good object." The good object — in this case, jazz — must not be thought about or questioned or doubted. It may, on the other hand, be able to withstand criticism or disparagement if criticism or disparagement serves to affirm to the group that the outsiders do not understand, thereby turning condemnation into praise and re-assuring the group about the value of the good object and of those dedicated to it.

The same process is operative when we insist upon sex's interest: Sex, if considered as a "good object," might punish us if we ask or think too much about it.

According to the joke, those who inquire about what jazz is — i.e., those who think about it — do not "get it." They will never get it, according to Armstrong, and, what is more, they *should* not get it.

Their efforts to get it (where "get it" means "comprehend it") make it impossible for them to get it (where "get it" means "partake in it") because their efforts to think about it threaten the group's possession of it.

The group seems to have a strong interest in *not* thinking about itself and its primary activity. If Armstrong is right, then jazz musicians and jazz aficionados do not think about what jazz is. I doubt this is true, but it is certainly true that, while playing jazz, one does not spend much time thinking about whether or not the music one is playing qualifies as jazz. To do so would be to disrupt the experience of playing, and, like the centipede who begins to wonder which foot to put out first, to trip oneself up.

These speculations may be applied to the hypothetical rejoinder about sex: "If you don't get it (where 'get it' means 'comprehend whether or why sex is interesting'), you will not get it (where 'get it' means 'get to have sexual activity or intercourse') because those who do have sexual activity intercourse might lose it if forced to think about it."

Why?

Might they lose their capacity to *do* it?

Might they lose interest in it?

There are, of course, important differences between playing jazz and thinking about jazz, between having sex and thinking about sex. For some reason, these differences are elided in the jokes and quips we have been discussing, which are, essentially, insistences that an activity will be ruined if it is thought about.

To think about sex's interest — rather than just assuming or believing that it is interesting — suggests that there is room for doubt about sex's ability to hold interest, or, put another way, our ability to hold interest in sex.

This room for doubt is *the same room* that is needed if there is to be interest.

Room for interest is coincidental with room for doubt.

But making room for interest, like making room for doubt, may conjure misgivings about the value of sex as well as all those activities related to sex and sexuality in which many of us find ourselves involved. Sex comprises, of course, far more than a loosely defined set of bodily activities: It is a vast human enterprise related to our identities, our relationships, our cultures and polities, our wish to find meaning in sexual attractiveness and engagement, our experiences of art, literature, poetry, history, mythology, and much more.

When we insist that something must not be thought about, we are consciously enabling the psychic mechanism of repression, since we are saying: "Certain thoughts must not be thought." Repression reveals the part of our ambivalence we wish to hide from ourselves and others: in this case, disinterest in, disdain for, even repulsion at sex.

As a musician, or former musician, I feel qualified to say that most musicians hold powerfully ambivalent feelings about music, often loving it, often hating it, sometimes dreading it, frequently refusing to listen to it at all, yet sometimes discovering in it something wonderful.

This idea may seem odd to those who watch live musical performances or who listen to musicians speak—and *lie*—about their lifelong, unwavering, and unequivocal love of music. The reality is much closer to Marianne Moore's famous poem about poetry and entitled, "Poetry," which begins:

"I, too, dislike it."

"There are things," Moore continues, "that are important beyond all / this fiddle."

And yet, it is also true that: "Reading it [...] with a perfect contempt for it, one / discovers in / it after all, a place for the genuine" (1994, 36).

15.

So when Wallace Shawn, an intelligent and admirable man in so many respects, writes an apologia for having written so much about sex, why is he unable or unwilling to address the question of whether sex is interesting?

Perhaps his own fascination with, boredom with, or misinterest in sex are kept out of sight, even for him, even from the start.

Or perhaps Shawn is afraid of the (Freudian) threat we've just discussed: "If you doubt the interest of sex, then you won't *get it* anymore." On this note, Shawn's essay does begin with an acknowledgment of his age (sixty-four, at the time of writing).

Shawn's tone is so friendly that it may appear humorless to take the essay apart claim by claim. And yet, his disarming style is involved in the subtlety with which he advances his claims.

He begins by explaining that he is not at all responsible for what he has written, but that, rather, he is a mere vessel for another voice, a voice that "contributes everything," while he contributes "nothing."

Rather, as a writer, he listens as a "voice [...] comes in through the window, whose words I write down in a state of weirded-out puzzlement, thinking, 'Jesus Christ, what is he saying?.'"

> When I try to define the voice, I say, weakly, "Oh, that's the unconscious," but I'm eventually forced to conclude that, if the unconscious has thoughts, it has to have heard these thoughts (or at least their constituent fragments) from human beings of some description. (2009, 157)

The unconscious, by definition, does not have "thoughts." We could debate the content of the unconscious, but no one would seriously defend the notion that it is, as Shawn implies, made up solely of overheard conversations or items one has read about or spoken of with others.

This seems to me to be a rather ineffective attempt on Shawn's part to distance himself from his own writing, to locate the "interest" of sex in other people, and to present himself as little more than a translator of the world's concerns, even if he has to locate those interests and those people, first, outside his window, then in his ear, and ultimately in his unconscious (about which he claims to be conscious).

Shawn's next line of argument is that "sex is shocking," that human beings do not typically imagine themselves as being involved with sex, but, rather, as being occupied with more "uniquely human" things, such as hailing a taxi or voting in an election. Instead, when he remembers or is made aware that he, too, engages in sex, he is unexpectedly reminded that

> my soul and body are capable of being totally swept up in a pursuit and an activity that pigs, flies, wolves, lions, and tigers also engage in, my normal picture of myself is violently disrupted. In other words, consciously, I am aware that I am a product of evolution, and I am part of nature. [...] Sex is "the environment" coming inside. (159–60)

It is worth remarking the sexual nature of Shawn's account of his own writing about sex. First, Shawn implies that he writes about sex so often because people and voices are always penetrating his body and his mind. Then, he defines the very fact of human sexuality as an act of penetration and disruption by "the environment" which "com[es] inside."

It is surprising that someone of Shawn's experience and intellect would genuinely find sex shocking, particularly for the reasons — which may not be the *real* reasons; only the ones you can write about in *Harper's Magazine* — Shawn sets forth. To be sure, there can be shocking moments in sex, moments of surprise, wonder, creativity, or even terror shared between sexual partners. These, however, are not typically moments of primitive animality, but the opposite: moments when people recognize themselves and each other and rediscover their capacities to create, or to fail to create, a human experience that is all their own.

With all due respect, the bulk of Shawn's essay is unremarkable. His final claim, however, is bizarre enough to deserve mention. Shawn writes that "sex seems capable of creating anarchy," and his defense of this point is that the *New York Times* does not print pictures of naked people.

Shawn asserts that "nudity somehow seems to imply that anything could happen" (162), and that this is why the staid and reliable *Times* could never publish nudes, as if doing so would create a sort of mass panic: Manhattanites bolting from their brownstones, tearing out each other's guts, copulating in a Bacchic frenzy.

The fantasy that underlies this absurd notion is, of course, an ancient, common, and, frankly, *boring* one, in which we may see the root of Shawn's fascination with sex. Shawn imagines that sex and nudity — nudity's relation to sex is never made clear, by the way — hold magical powers, powers that are not precisely preternatural but, rather, Natural with a capital "N."

The idea — one that has been heard since the birth of Attic tragedy and likely long before — is that sex is so Natural that it drives us "wild." When we enter the "wilderness" of sex, we leave our cities, our manners, our clothing, and all that represents our civilized identities behind.

Thus, "sex really is a nation of its own," for Shawn. "Those whose allegiance is given to sex at a certain moment withdraw their loyalty temporarily from other powers. It's a symbol of the possibility that we might all defect for one reason or another from the obedient columns in which we march" (163).

But if sex is one power, one order, among many, then there is no reason to believe that, in the "Nation of Sex," we have any fewer responsibilities or any fewer "obedient columns" in which to march. Indeed, it seems a rather tragic fantasy to believe that we must leave our selves behind in order to find our selves and our Natural interest elsewhere, in a foreign nation we may visit briefly, but where we can never reside.

16.

In one of the most memorable pieces of writing in all of Continental philosophy, *Either/Or, Volume 1: The Rotation Method,* Søren Kierkegaard offers an exposition of what would otherwise be a boring distinction between two types of "*rotation*": (1) rotation as endless change, and (2) rotation oriented to and limited by the aim of cultivation, as in agriculture.

In the first, the "vulgar and inartistic method," we find Shawn's and others' attitudes toward sex, as we are drawn to repeated "change[s] of field" (Kierkegaard 1946, 25). The allure of sex, we may extrapolate, is the allure of movement, novelty, change of scenery. In practice, this explains why sex so often compels people to seek new partners, new positions, new roles, and the like.

There is a childish quality to this method of "rotation," for it forgets, and keeps forgetting, again and again, that such change is superficial. It is, moreover, "supported by illusion": specifically, the illusion that the next change will be more meaningful than the last. "One tires of living in the country," writes Kierkegaard,

> and moves to the city; one tires of living in one's native land, and travels abroad; one is *europamüde* [Euro-weary], and goes to America, and so on; finally one indulges in a sentimental hope of endless journeyings from star to star. [...] One tires of porcelain dishes and eats on silver; one tires of

> silver and turns to gold; one burns half of Rome to get an idea of the burning of Troy. (25)

Such change is repetitive — as oxymoronic as that may sound — because change becomes a constant, a compulsion. The compulsion is supported by illusion because the change involved actually signifies the absence of, even the defiance of, change.

The illusion that supports such change, along with the idea of sex being "a nation of its own," is the illusion that, by changing some more or less superficial aspects of our lives, or by engaging briefly in an activity that bears an unclear relation to the rest of our daily activities, we will re-create or re-discover what is elusive but essential: our interest in living.

As a young man and undergraduate student, I found Kierkegaard engaging and liberating, in large part because of the essay cited above, in which he dares to claim that the history of the world is boring. I suppose this idea, when considered at an age when one is told one must be interested in *everything* if one is not to be a boor — which makes real interest impossible — came as something of a relief.

"Boredom is the root of all evil," writes Kierkegaard. "What wonder, then, that the world goes from bad to worse, and that evils increase more and more, as boredom increases."

> The history of this can be traced from the very beginning of the world. The gods were bored, and so they created man. Adam was bored because he was alone, and so Eve was created. Thus boredom entered the world, and increased in proportion to the increase of population. Adam was bored alone; then Adam and Eve were bored together; then Adam and Eve and Cain and Abel were bored *en famille*; then the populations of the world increased and the peoples were bored *en masse*. To divert themselves they conceived the idea of constructing a tower high enough to reach the heavens. This idea is itself as boring as the tower was high [...]. The nations were scattered over the earth, just as people now travel

> abroad, but they continue to be bored. [...] And is anything being done now? [...] It is proposed to call a constitutional assembly. Can anything more tiresome be imagined, both for the participants themselves, and for those who have to hear and read about it? It is proposed to improve the financial condition of the state by practicing economy. What could be more tiresome? (22–23)

17.

These reflections lead me to conclude with what will be considered an unlikely and perhaps unfortunate topic on the subject of sexual interest: US President Donald Trump.

Having read and studied much of what there is to read and study about the election that brought this man to power, I have concluded that, more likely than accounts of the "forgotten, white, lower-middle class," millions of Americans were desperately bored, so they elected Trump.

Trump was and is the bloated, overwhelming signifier, pointing to nothing, with which half of America (or more than half) became fascinated.

To presume that Trump could have risen to power only by force of American racism, sexism, classism, bigotry, and other forms of malice would be to neglect the power of misinterest, of boredom and fascination, to influence human conduct.

The power of misinterest can hardly be overestimated; it often exceeds the powers of love and hate.

The problem is that Americans have been told for quite a long time that they must be interested in things in which they are not interested; indeed, in things that are boring, such as American government and politics.

Without any clear means of making government and politics interesting, people like Donald Trump, Rush Limbaugh, and others fulfill an important psychic and social need: They resolve the dissonance between (a) the expectation that government and politics be interesting and the reality that (b) without outlandishness and grotesquerie, government and politics are boring.

They do not make politics interesting, but they collude in the destruction of what precious little is potentially interesting about government and politics in order to magnify both the boring and the fascinating.

Put another way, millions of Americans became fascinated by Trump because Trump reflected and represented their boredom. Trump was and is the raging child in the grocery store, howling at the excruciating pain of his boredom.

Trump, the bored child, became fascinating to millions of bored American adults because he was childish enough or honest enough or naïve enough to admit how bored he was by all workings, principles, and norms of humanity, law, government, and politics.

The Democratic Party has not yet caught on to this.

It may be time for liberals to launch a years-long campaign aimed solely at convincing people that government and politics will hold for them limited, if any, interest.

Then, if people still felt obliged to inform themselves or to vote, they would at least not expect to be titillated, fascinated by the process.

The same may be said for sex.

Imagine the quantity of human suffering, frustration, and disappointment that could be relieved if it were announced with any degree of authority that sex, after all, had been discovered to be *not necessarily interesting* and, more to the point, that if one did not find great interest in sex, whether one enjoyed it or partook in sex a great deal, one need not consider oneself or one's sexual relationships "dysfunctional," nor need one seek psychological "treatment" for any "disorder."

Perhaps, someone will say, our sex lives and our democracy would suffer terribly if we followed this path. Perhaps sexual participation rates would drop, just as voter turnout rates would fall from fifty-five percent—already an unimpressive figure by any standard—to, say, twenty-five. Perhaps the pretense of interest is somehow essential to retaining critical participation in sex, politics, shopping, and the like, without which the society, the economy, and the species would suffer.

I doubt it. Instead, I wonder if we might not take a step toward confronting the truth about interest, toward recognizing how stuck we are in cycles of misinterest, boredom, and fascination, offering some chance to some daring few to break out of the unsatisfying rotations and compulsive repetitions of sex, politics, even daily life, itself.

A Dream of Guilt

My sister has killed herself and has left, beside her body, a "test" of some kind, in her bed, all bloody.

It is a revealing test to be sure, a litmus test of sorts, but not a test of her. Rather, it is a test of us all, a test that will prove our guilt.

My father is as nonchalant as could be.

In fact, he is most concerned that I see a pillowcase on which has been written, in permanent marker, the following words, deemed to be of great importance and effectuating something of a double-bind:

> *If Matthew comes home, throw this pillowcase away immediately.*

We are staying in a ritzy house in a tropical place whose name sounds like, but is nowhere near and nothing like, Saint Tropez.

My mother wakes up hot and sweaty from the effort of sleeping.

She is frightened by her state and I comfort her as if she were my wife.

I have a close relationship of a romantic nature with a man who plays the xylophone beautifully.

He and I are concerned that people will see us together without our clothes on.

He empties the garbage cans musically, then returns to his xylophone and plays, "I'll be Your Mirror," but, in doing so, makes it clear that the song is not intended for me.

Thus, as I say goodnight, I leave him a small charm, a silver teddy bear, on the side table, for I will never see him again.

The television in my room announces, cryptically: "'Do Not Inform' is a penis cancer agent."

"Remember," it cautions ominously, "D.N.I.P.C.A."

"Do Not Inform" is, itself, a well-known psychiatric condition, as dangerous as penis cancer.

"I have had both," I say to myself; I thought I had fully recovered.

Now, I cry out, to myself and others, "I have them again!" but no one hears.

Instead, my mother sobs in the living room.

I rush in to sympathize with her, but this time she responds with an accusation: "You have been terrible," she says.

Horrified at her suggestion — that my sister's death is my fault — I fall silent.

She mistakes my silence for the desire to officially change my name.

My sister officially changed her name several times throughout her life.

"Now I suppose you'll change yours!" she spews with a glower.

I cannot follow her logic, and yet I feel that what she says rings true.

She lunges at me violently.

I am shocked and scream but, oddly, I feel freer than before, because now I am face to face with my accuser.

I begin to build up confidence but am repeatedly assaulted by terrible things: a phone call telling me my "timesheet is messed up," a tax consultant informing me I owe $30,000, instructions from the intercom to climb the impossible staircase that is really a treadmill.

Confused, I suddenly remark my wife's books on the side table where, earlier, I had laid the teddy bear charm.

At this moment, I realize that I am dreaming, and in spite of the nightmarish qualities of the dream, I decide to remain within it, or I dream that I make this decision, so that I can do whatever I please without consequence.

My most immediate and overwhelming desire is to kiss someone, so I do.

As I do, I pause for a moment, to reassure myself that the person I am kissing is, indeed, my wife.

Eros and Hatred in Three Groups

— Group 1 —

1.

I recently returned from serving as a Fulbright Specialist in pedagogy and curricular development in Singapore. My task was to assist a private university in their efforts to enhance critical thinking, creativity, reflectiveness, and autonomous questioning among students.

Part of my work including facilitating several lengthy workshops with faculty and student-tutors in which we discussed these outcomes, their meaning, and the many forces that can get in their way.

In several of these workshops, I devoted a considerable amount of time to the topic of group dynamics, since classes, study groups, peer-mentoring sessions, and even universities themselves all involve groups, and since group forces may exert tremendous power over group members, often to the detriment of critical thinking, creativity, reflectiveness, and autonomy.

For portions of these workshops, I introduced a modified, highly abbreviated, and relatively benign version of the Tavistock method of group study and experience known best via the work conducted by the A.K. Rice Institute and the writings of W.R. Bion (2001).

The most basic yet most essential insight of this area of group psychology is that "groups" are more than bunches of individuals, and more than the collectivity they form. Once a group is formed, it takes on a psychic life of its own — fueled primarily by members' externalized unconscious needs, desires, and fears.

The banality "the whole is greater than the sum of its parts" does not do this insight justice, for the group is both greater than *and* distinct from the "whole" that is greater than the sum of its constituent members. The group is or becomes a semi-autonomous (i.e., influenced but not determined by any single individual, or even by all of the group members' conscious wishes) force, which, in turn, acts upon group members individually and collectively.

Large groups may possess a massive aspect — as in: an aspect of the "mass" — but even they are both more and less than a mass. The "face" of this group is not that of an individual, nor is it "ourselves, sounding ourselves," at least not precisely. Instead, "There are not leaves enough to cover the face / it wears." It governs us and then is "nowhere again, away and away." It is "never the face / That hermit on reef sable would have seen, / Never the naked politician taught / By the wise," only the face of the invisible, colossal group (Stevens 1990, 206).

I sometimes find myself imagining the group as a kind of cloud, in both a basic and more contemporary sense. The trick, when in groups, is to be aware that we sit amidst a cloud that contains powerful psychic charges, and to attempt to make that cloud — and its changing colors and tone and charges and movements and which is presently thundering, et cetera, et cetera. — more visible and comprehensible to group members.

This aim, of facilitating awareness of the group — which is to say the "group-level" of experience — is the primary aim of the activities concerned with group-dynamics mentioned above.

2.

In the modified version of the group activity I introduce, I inform group members of the nature and objectives of the activity up front, I counsel them a bit about the theory of groups with which I am operating, and I warn them that I, as a group facilitator, will be attuned to the group level of experience — and not to individual group members or sub-groups — with the ultimate goal of drawing their attention to the group level of experience.

This also means, I inform them, that I may behave somewhat differently than a traditional moderator of a discussion or leader of a workshop. I ask them to consider their primary "work task" to be to reflect upon and discuss what is happening at the group-level experience in real time. I even write this "work task" on the board, for reasons that will become clear shortly.

Then, I usually ask if everyone feels comfortable with the activity or if any questions remain before starting. When all are ready, I say simply, "Okay, let's begin."

Typically, as I fall silent, the group falls silent for several minutes as they try to figure out what to do in this unique situation. They may be trying to figure out how to organize themselves, how to speak to other group members, whether or not they really want to be a part of the group and its work, or whether they can tolerate the anxiety of being in an ambiguous and, to some degree, leaderless group.

Frequently, the tension of silence is broken by an individual who asks, perhaps on behalf of or in service of the fledgling group, if I can re-explain everything about the activity: its work, its goal, and what members are "supposed to do."

This presents an immediate challenge the group facilitator, who must decide what the question really expresses and how it relates to the life of the group. Some facilitators simply remain silent. I usually do not.

Every group is different, but fairly commonly I find myself saying something like, "I wonder if this request for clarification on behalf of the group is actually something else entirely."

You see, to do this work, although you are sincerely trying to help, you have to be willing to be a bit evasive, even, perhaps, a bit of an asshole, like a cross between a Yoda and that guidance counselor who thinks he is too smart to be a guidance counselor and so tries to do psychotherapy with children when they only need some form to be signed.

The response is not meant to be frustrating, but it is often taken to be so. After all, the objectives and nature of the activity were explained clearly and at length; the "work task" of the group is even written clearly on the board.

The group, then, is not really asking for clarification but for something else. The group is using the voice of a willing member to test the facilitator, to see to what degree it can become a dependent group: dependent upon the facilitator to do all the work for the group.

Refusing to answer this question directly, then, is a way of telling the group that, as a facilitator, I am not going to collude with their effort to make the group dependent upon me, although it may very well become a dependent group anyway.

3.

The most extreme example of a dependent group I had ever encountered was the first group in Singapore with whom I introduced this exercise. They did something I had never experienced before: They immediately disintegrated. It was as if an alarm bell had gone off.

Within seconds of beginning, all group members pulled their chairs back from the circle, took out their mobile phones, and paired off into small groups of two or three, chatting about everyday things: gossip, news, breakfast, and the like.

This continued for twenty minutes with only one interruption: One group member shouted over the din, "This is great; can we do this all day?" at which group chuckled.

The immediate collapse of the group, as a group, was shocking. My own experience was one of amazement, but also frustration, and, eventually, anger.

The group had refused to be born, had refused, right from the start, to become a group. The only thing that group members did together was to disband or abort the group, rejecting its potentiality, never giving it a chance to be, never giving themselves or me a chance to experience it.

Eventually, when I became convinced that we would, indeed, "do this all day" absent any intervention from me, I somewhat reluctantly said: "I wonder why the group killed itself."

The response to this somewhat mysterious comment by group members was to all assert and concur that, absent clear directions from me, they could not do anything other than what they did. That is, their actions held no meaning and were the only, the natural, and the inevitable outcome of the activity.

What is more, they did not understand the meaning of my statement, and they rejected the premise that there was or could have been a group to kill. They made it clear that they would continue to reject tasks that were ambiguous and unstructured, in large part because they saw in them no point or purpose. I had designed these tasks, in the view of the majority, to be deliberately frustrating, depriving, and withholding.

While this group represents something near to one extremity of a disorganized and helplessly dependent group, a group that rejects even the work of becoming a group, the experience holds an insight into the accusation of withholding.

4.

Quite often, group members will accuse group facilitators of withholding the assistance, the "answers," or the support necessary for the group to function.

Such accusations contain considerable emotional valences: rage, sadness, terror, feelings of abandonment, and more.

In a dyadic (one person to one person) psychotherapeutic encounter, an accusation that the analyst is withholding something from the patient may be interpreted as a manifestation of the transference, which means simply that the patient is transferring or projecting into the analyst's silence the meanings, emotions, and understandings associated with another silence that resides at least partly in the patient's unconscious. The patient has formed a schema or paradigm about silence, absence, neglect, withholding, or deprivation that is activated by the analyst's behavior and that arises in the psyche of the patient when the analyst's behavior permits.

What struck me about the group referred to above, and then about subsequent groups with which I interacted on this trip, was that the accusation of withholding may be more helpfully understood along different lines when dealing with groups.

In these cases, the accusation of withholding seemed to be less a matter of projecting group members' prior experiences or fantasies onto me or onto the group, and, more fundamentally, a matter of the projection the group's own withholding behavior.

That is, it was the group that was withholding itself from itself. It was group members who were refusing to share, to be a part of, or to contribute themselves to the group in ways that might have given the group something with which to work.

In a different language, we might say that it was not I who was withholding the nourishment needed for the group to thrive but the group, itself.

This insight, of course, even when I suggested it to the group in a way that the group could ingest, could not be recognized by the group.

This method of understanding the meaning of the accusation of withholding resonates to some degree with Harry Guntrip's notion of the "schizoid compromise" (1992), for group members split off and withhold valuable aspects of themselves from the group, while, at the same time, projecting onto the group disavowed impulses and emotions.

In many groups, a bargain is struck such that group activity will be, of necessity, empty, draining, and meaningless, even to the degree that the group experiences a good deal of anxiety about its own annihilation. This anxiety, then, seems to be more tolerable than the anxiety provoked by not withholding selves from the group in the ways called for by the group's work.

5.

Of course, we are all schizoid.

There is a *healthy* splitting and preservation of a part of the self, a part not available to others.

Retaining a secret part or parts of the self, what Winnicott calls our "incommunicado" elements (1965, 187), is necessary if we wish to remain subjects, to assure contact with ourselves in difficult circumstances, and to exercise reflective autonomy and agency in groups.

— Group 2 —

I.

At a recent panel discussion at the meeting of the Association for the Psychoanalysis of Culture and Society, one participant made a comparison between the stigma associated with the slang term for mental illness, "crazy," and the more powerful stigma of "the *n*-word."

In making her point, however, she did not say "the *n*-word," but, rather, used the *n*-word.

The group organized itself around this utterance.

It took its new purpose to be that of sharing experiences of race-, gender-, sex-, and sexuality-oriented victimization. These were overwhelmingly the kinds of events that we now class, for better or for worse, as "micro-aggressions": subtle verbal slights, ignorant and callous remarks. For example, a black person is questioned about the texture and style of her hair, or a person's gender-identity is presumed based on physical appearance alone.

Group members responded to these narratives with sympathetic sighs and nodding, but also with wringing hands and winces, visible reactions of pain and even guilt, an important matter which I discuss below. In any case, the reactions of group members affirmed to the group that these experiences were important and painful. The utterance, in this sense, was the catalyst that gave the group a chance to form an identity and a belief-system or ideology.

It did not appear that the participant who used the *n*-word meant it as an attack, although she later admitted that she knew it might be "provocative." In such cases, one can often rightly assume that the individual is hoping (perhaps unconsciously) to draw the ire of the group or, at the very least, to ensure that her individual contribution becomes central to the group's life and activity.

Somewhat surprisingly, this participant was never attacked in a personal way by the group. If she succeeded in making her utterance central to the group's short life, the group responded by making her continuing presence — including her later comments and attempts at clarification — seem utterly irrelevant.

The utterance allowed many group members to forge identifications with those who suffer the racism, hatred, and degradation associated with and represented by the *n*-word. Through this identification with what might be called the (victim) "ego-ideal" (see Freud 1959), group members bonded with each other.

At the most patent level, the group found a way to change its function, which was initially to discuss an academic question having little or nothing to do with victimization.

At a deeper level, the group found that it could achieve what all groups seek to achieve, an experience wherein members are submerged into a group that feels larger than life and is fantasied to be harmonious, perfect, and even, in some sense, immortal.

This is the coming-together dynamic of groups, the group's embrace of the group, which is not the same thing as the group's embrace of its members, as a collectivity or as individuals. Let us call it the *primary erotic activity of groups.*

2.

Erotic activity in groups defends against the fear of fragmentation or disintegration, a fear that has more than a whiff of early (infantile, childhood) loss.

It may be understood as an attempt to recreate in the group what Winnicott refers to as a "holding environment" (1965), the earliest form of connection between infant and caregiver, where, instead of bounded persons, relationships, and difference, there is unity, communion, and an experience of merger in which a corporate strength or power may be found.

"There is no such thing as a baby," Winnicott famously quipped (1992, 99); there is only a baby-caregiver dyad, fused together by Eros, among other things.

A group's erotic activity, then, is inseparable from its need to survive: Once "born," the group does not want to "die."

At the same time, of course, individual group members do not want to "die" by being subsumed by or swallowed up by the group. The ambivalence — and, sometimes, outright contradiction — between these dual ends and dual anxieties, constitutes a good deal of the psychic activity of groups.

This means, of course, that the terms "erotic" and "Eros" must be read broadly and not strictly in line with the "Eros" of Plato, Sigmund Freud, Herbert Marcuse, or any other individual thinker.

What is truly "erotic," in the sense intended to describe the activity of this group and others, is not the sublimated sexual activity or fantasy life of the group — although this remains important — but the continuation of the life of the group, the consolidation of the group around basic assumptions, beliefs, and fantasies, and the formation of a group identity that offers a form of psychic support (if members align themselves with it adequately).

In this particular group, members' preoccupation with telling tales of victimization was both erotic and regressed: regressed toward a paranoid stance in which the conflict between identifications with victim and victimizer was intensified.

The aggression occasioned by this paranoid stance was only partly directed "outside." That is, the participant who uttered the *n*-word was not "cast out," nor did group members wish *only* to split up the world into those outside the group setting and those inside it.

Rather, the tales of victimization told by group members elicited affective reactions — the hand-wringing and wincing described above — that expressed not only the fact that these experiences cause victims to feel diminished to the extent that they accept and internalize the attribution implied by the words or actions of the victimizer. Rather, members simultaneously took on the guilt of the victimizer.

To the extent that this interpretation is accurate —and it may not be — it would imply that the group's activity was not split *so simply* as one might think, e.g., 'The inside (the group) is good and the outside (the world) is bad.'

In a more complex way, members evinced hostility and aggression toward members' own inner victimizers, the parts of themselves identified with victimizers.

The group was able to recognize that the "outside" was also inside, in the sense that members could not or did not wish to fully distance themselves from guilt for victimization.

Perhaps the group felt that its activity would help excise these inner victimizers. But, of course, this kind of activity is, itself, victimizing.

That is, the parts of ourselves that identify with victimizers — which is to say: that see ourselves in them, and see them in ourselves — cannot be gotten rid of so easily, mainly because of the obvious paradox: Attempts to destroy our victimizer-selves are acts of victimization themselves, as parts of ourselves come under attack. Thus, when we attack our victimizer-selves we are, at the same time, identified with and acting on behalf of our victimizer-selves. Therefore, we are expressing erotic impulses toward the parts of ourselves identified with victimizers, and these, too, become part of the psychic life of the individual or the group.

3.

After being patient for a long time, a senior member of the Association was given the chance to speak and managed to get out only eight words ("I teach at a large state university and —") before being interrupted by several others who informed him that he was derailing the group's activity.

These persons, including the group's leaders, reminded him of the need to "stay with what was happening" in the group.

This individual spoke in a calm voice with little emotion.

If it was inferred from his affect that he would not "stay with" the group's primary activity, it was because it was clear that he was not likely to testify to an experience of victimization.

Worse, he was going to offer a thought.

The majority of group members, at that moment, did not want to depart from the activity of testifying about victimization and certainly did not wish to think, for several reasons, the most important of which is the possibility that his thought would have called the group's attention to the fact that they were speaking about discrimination and victimization, but were really interested in exploring ways to identify with their victimizer-selves.

Testimonials of being victimized were covers for a different sort of activity: the group's coming together as a group of victims who victimized each other's inner victimizers.

4.

It seems worth pointing out that, at the beginning of this group's time together, a short speech was given about fluidity in sex- and gender-identity and, in what has become a familiar practice, all members of the group were told to state our names, followed by our preferred pronouns:

Hi, I'm Matt: He, Him, His.
Hi, I'm Zelda: They, Them, Their.
Hi, I'm Ty: Ze, Zir, Zirs.

While understandable, this exercise strikes me as a very unfortunate way to begin group conversations.

The breathless conjunction of names with strings of pronouns makes it difficult to recall anyone's proper name, much less each person's preferred pronouns. So, after this exercise has been completed, group members may have succeeded in revealing aspects of their individual identities to the group, but, ultimately, have partaken in a group ritual that may hold deleterious consequences for productive group work.

As might be expected, group members quickly forgot how to address each other, and, thus, the conversation became more abstract, passive, and fearful than necessary, as in:

> *Something said a few minutes ago by, erm—sorry I forget your name—in response to the earlier, um, comment made by—made a few minutes ago on the topic of structural violence, was—interesting, in my opinion.*

Perhaps this blockage of communication was, or is, an unconscious goal.

It is also possible, if not likely, that *not all* members of all groups wish to announce the pronouns associated with their sex- or gender-identities, whether they are consciously aware of their aversion or not.

The idea driving the practice of announcing pronouns is, of course, that having one's sex- or gender-identity mistaken can be painful. The practice is intended to prevent this.

But beneath the fear of being mistaken lies a conviction that announcing one's preferred pronouns cannot or *should not* be painful, or, at least, that it is less painful than being mistaken.

Put another way, the activity suggests that, even if someone may wish to abstain—for whatever reason—from announcing his/her/their/zirs pronouns, no one *should* wish to abstain from the ritual because the ritual, itself, is fantasized to possess magical properties by which shame is transformed into pride. By enforcing this ritual (quite undemocratically), the group insists that members *should* be proud of their sex- and gender-identities.

A desire not to announce one's pronouns to a group would be understood by the group as a *betrayal,* in both senses of the word:

1. betrayal as contravention of a group norm, in this case, the norm of showing pride, even if the person does not actually *feel* pride, and
2. betrayal as revelation of the individual's emotional and intellectual reality and presence as an individual, perhaps with complex and ambivalent feelings about his/her/their/zirs own sex and gender identity, and not merely as a member of a group that insists on performances of pride.

Not to pronounce one's pronouns betrays the group because abstention introduces doubt, not only about the strength of the ties that bind group members together — including their beliefs, their dedication to their rituals, their fantasies of abandonment of individuality for the group, et cetera — but about the core conviction that the group is capable of mobilizing aggression to protect members from shame.

5.

Many people struggle mightily with their sexes, genders, and sexualities. Many queer persons face enormous challenges in societies and cultures where cis-gender identity and heterosexuality are still the norms, where "deviations" from these norms are stigmatized, and where such stigmatizations are internalized in the form of shame.

Yet, there are different methods that we can employ in the struggle against shame. Insisting that, instead of shame, we feel pride, is one. There is no need to feel pride about one's sex, gender, race, or sexuality, for instance, unless there is, first, shame, or the possibility of shame.

In pronouncing pronouns, people announce their pride and insist that others do so as well, regardless of whether that pride is genuine or, beneath the active performance of pride, there is a reservoir of shame that must not be acknowledged.

This reservoir of shame is projected into the group, and is related to ambivalently: It is both depended upon and attacked.

Shame is inextricably linked to the part of the self that identifies with the victimizing other. To attempt to eliminate shame from members of a group is to supplant internal defenses against victimization (identification with the aggressor) with group-based defenses (identification with the group, which may be aggressive, itself).

Thus, the bargain is this: The group will provide members with identity-support and will protect members to some degree from experiences of shame, so long as the member attacks those aspects of his/her/their/zirs individual identities that do not accord with the group's basic beliefs, fantasies, and assumptions.

The connection, then, between the preliminary activity of pronouncing pronouns and the later erotic/aggressive activity of the group is this: The group was "born" in a ritual whose emotional meaning was: "All group members must be on guard against their own feelings of shame, which is to say: against their own internal victimizers. But, at the same time, we must bring to the group our shame, in the form of pronouncing pronouns of pride, and as a part of the narratives of victimization and their impacts, so that shame can be attacked."

Put another way, the group decided that it could and should victimize the victimizers, both within and without.

In sum, the group did not regress *because* of an outside threat, represented by one member's use of the *n*-word or the possibility of a group member misgendering another. Rather, the group seized opportunities to victimize itself, in a manner of speaking, in a forum where group members would not have to become aware of this activity.

— Group 3 —

I.

Each year, I teach an advanced seminar in psychoanalytic political theory. The course examines hatred, among other things, as a central dynamic in the life of families, organizations, and groups.

The participants in the seminar reflect upon our own group experience — our own thoughts, feelings, and experiences as they arise in the group — as part of our work.

This "group encounter" aspect of the course demands that my role as professor include some of the work of a psychodynamically-sensitive "group facilitator," and that students, too, become conscious of their dual roles as students and as group members.

There is a particular kind of "Eros" running through any college class, even more so for a course on a subject of emotional intensity. The desire — shared by professors and students — to "love" the course and to "love" one another is always there.

In this case, the class was already close-knit, comprising eighteen students who had enrolled in an undergraduate "learning community," and who had taken a number of courses together for the past three and a half years.

The course group had already reached certain conclusions about hatred, conclusions which I believed to be reasonably well-founded. For instance, we had spent some time reflecting upon the way hatred can be used to distance the self from internal bad (hated) objects.

We had arrived at a shared understanding of the need for hated objects, too, since, if we, following Otto Kernberg, associate hatred with rage, then by taking on the badness of our rage, hated objects permit us to experience our rage without experiencing our hatred and, therefore, without experiencing shame or guilt.

Likewise, we had come to a tenuous agreement regarding the transformative nature of hatred and the way that it often behooves the hating person or group to transform an object into something *more,* not less, hateful, so that the hatred already felt is better justified.

2.

Rather late in the semester — which, until then, had proceeded more or less uneventfully — a student announced abruptly:

I really hate the kids in my classes.

It was an odd statement, and not germane to our discussion.

It was also quite clear, from her body language, her gaze, and the direction in which she spoke, that she was not talking about "her classes" in an abstract or general sense but was, in fact, referring to a particular and identifiable sub-group of students in our class.

The students to whom she referred were present at the time, although they were not paying attention to her: an important dynamic that likely contributed to her feelings of hatred.

The student continued:

Sometimes people are just so stupid. I hate stupid people. So, I guess I am like a Nazi or something?

This student's announcement of her hatred, combined with the complex question of whether her hatred made her bad and hateful — which was at least part of the emotional meaning of "like a Nazi"— proved challenging for me and for the group.

Nearly all group members were aware that the comment was directed at a small number of readily identifiable members of the group. Some squirmed in discomfort.

The student was saying that she hated *those students right there,* and not just a little. She "really" hated them, perhaps in the way Nazis "really" hated Jews, homosexuals, Roma, and others.

She was also saying that she really hated the group, as a whole, and that she really hated me, as the group's facilitator, for causing her or permitting her to feel hatred and, what is worse, for putatively suggesting to her that she should feel "like a Nazi" for harboring hatred.

3.

My sense was that the student's comment was intended to accomplish several things at once.

First, and most obviously, she wished to vent hateful feelings toward a certain sub-group of students in the class, students who often derailed our progress with off-hand comments, noise, laughter, and other disruptions. These students also seemed to make other group members feel frustrated at not being attended to or heard.

This student also wished to push the limits of the group and to test my limits as a facilitator. She wished to see if we could tolerate an explicit announcement of hatred in a course in part about hatred, or if we would shut down the dialogue, mobilize aggression (and potentially hatred) against her, and collapse the openness that had thus far characterized our discussions.

I believe she knew we would not retaliate in this way, that it was "safe," at least in one sense, for her to announce her hatred. That is, it would have been extremely unlikely for anyone to have answered the student's rhetorical question about being like a Nazi in the affirmative — which I confess to having had the urge to do — by saying, for instance: "Yes, your hatred makes you like a Nazi." In some way, it did.

At the time of her comment, the sub-group of unruly students were again talking among themselves, not paying enough attention to her to notice that they were being named as hated objects, which, of course, only confirmed their hateful aspect in the eyes of some group members.

The behavior of the sub-group therefore was a predictable and convenient evidentiary hearing, by which the student was able to offer proof that her hatred was justified. This dynamic is by no means unknown to those who study victimization: The victimized persons, caught or recalled in the very act of being victimized, are seen in moments of degradation or diminishment, and are then regarded as degraded or diminished persons, unworthy of care and deserving only of further victimization.

What I found most fascinating was that the student's announcement of hatred had an impact on all members of the group *except* for the sub-group at which it was aimed, which might be said in another way: She instilled in others something of her experience, recruiting the majority of group members against the sub-group and asking them to share with her the burden of her hatred while in the presence of the hated sub-group.

It would not be at all surprising to me if this result was intended by the student: that her comment, appropriately timed, would coalesce the majority of the group around her hate.

Rejecting many of the complexities and conclusions reached in the course-group, the student offered a proposal, a kind of bargain, to the group:

> *If what we have learned is right, then my feelings of hatred mean I hate myself. But I am not like a Nazi, so I should not hate myself. Since I should not hate myself, I refuse to accept responsibility for my hatred. And yet I still hate. You can join me in my hatred and, since you are no more Nazis than I, you, too, will not have to experience yourselves as hateful, which means you, too, will not be forced to confront the hatred within yourselves. The idea that we could be involved with anything here, in this group, that resembles Nazis is absurd.*

She was asking, then, for support in identifying with her victimizer-self and to be able to survive this identification emotionally, both as an individual and as a group member. These are not unhealthy or unreasonable things to ask. And yet, she was asking, in an aggressive way, something that the group could not provide, even if they had tried: that the group make her feelings of hatred tolerable to herself.

4.

After she spoke, I felt it was necessary to let the group contemplate what had happened. I, too, needed time to think about it, so I remained silent for several moments.

The extremity of her simile — "like a Nazi" — suggested that, for her, the emotional tension produced in the group was considerable. The group had put her on the "wrong" side, the Nazi side, and she needed to get herself back to the "right" side.

She used the group, and the sub-group of students, then, to reject much of the substance of the course and to place an emotional burden — virtually an ultimatum — on the group as a whole, which was the burden of reconciling her own emotional dilemma. The group had made her feel shame for feeling hate, even though we had explicitly discussed the reality of hate and had tried to establish an environment in which hate could be recognized and dealt with maturely, as it is always a potential for persons and groups.

To the extent that she was seeking absolution for her hatred, I could not provide it, mainly because that would lie beyond the boundaries of my roles as facilitator and professor. Likewise, the group did not defend or console her. Perhaps this was because such a request for absolution, if indeed there was one, was framed in such a way that in order to grant it, we would have had to become complicit in her hatred and in her implicitly hateful denouncement of the group and of our work together.

It may be that the student who announced her hatred did so because the alternative was for her to feel fractured, disintegrated, or annihilated, or for her to fracture, disintegrate, or annihilate the group in some other, less reparable, and more terrifying way — terrifying, at least, in her imagination and fantasy.

In any case, the student's announcement returns us to the idea of using aggression to defend against shame.

Consider the similarities between group members who withhold themselves from groups only to aggressively accuse the group or its facilitator of withholding and depriving them, persons who utter the *n*-word at academic conferences or otherwise aim to "provoke" the group, and split off and hated subgroup of students in a college course.

While these persons and groups disrupt the group's real work, they behave as if it is their function to sustain group life, without which there would be no group at all. They take their task to be a survival task, one of barely being. They provide reliable backstops against utter aimlessness, chaos, or group dissolution in the sense that the group can always turn to them to organize its activity around aggression or hate. In this sense, hate contributes, in a primitive but perhaps underappreciated way, to the erotic life of the group.

5.

Of course, as both a group member and the group's facilitator, I had to consider the student's comment in the context of my own feelings about her and about the group, which is a matter akin to analyzing the countertransference in psychoanalysis and is, unfortunately, too complex to examine at length here.

Nevertheless, it remains true that, in spite of a very difficult moment of hatred announced, and in spite of the fact that we could have very well devolved into extreme conflict, the group remained together and even remained, in some important sense, *unchanged*.

If I am honest, I believe this lack of change was a source of relief for me, since, at the time, it seemed to me that the group's emotional survival was being held in the balance.

My feelings of relief may very well make me *complicit* with conservative and regressive forces in the group, such as the desire not to change, not to learn, and not to grow from new experience.

Perhaps predictably, while I was contemplating this, laughter and irrelevant chatter from the disruptive sub-group of students distracted me and the rest of the students until our time was up.

A Dream of Teaching

A student from a course taught several years ago approaches me on a Manhattan street with an essay in hand.

She has an excuse for not turning in the essay on time.

Her excuse is "memory loss from Lupus."

But, she explains, she did not want to say this out loud in class, and so she is only bringing it up now, years later, in private.

May she still turn in her essay?

"Yes, of course," I say.

And then I feel the strong impulse to add:

"You can always tell me — but of course you do not have to tell me — about how you are feeling."

Suddenly, her eyes change.

She suspects something about this statement and her doubt rebounds upon me in such a way that I, too, question its motive and its sincerity.

She says, forcefully: "You are bullshit."

I reply: "*You* are bullshit."

As we part, I have a warm, comforting feeling that, in spite of our mutual suspicions to the contrary, I am a good person.

Civilizing Ironies

1.

The question, "How civilized are we?" holds several meanings. One meaning is: "Where can we direct our hatred?"

If we declare ourselves "uncivilized," we can hate human nature. Or, since all of us began as rather uncivilized creatures, we can hate the children we once were.

If we are "civilized," but anxious and depressed because of it, we can hate society and authority for making us so.

That is, if we are seeking suitable containers for hatred and self-hatred, then the only intolerable answer to the question of our degree of civilization would be: "The world is very civilized and everyone is thoroughly content."

Albeit a pleasant thought, this statement is not true. And if it were, it would seriously complicate our ability to manage our "uncivilized" emotions and impulses.

The noun "civilization" comes to us from the French Enlightenment (*civilisation*), after the verb "to civilize" had arisen from the adjective "civil." In this way, the very concept of "civilization" is inextricable from the "civilizing" projects of the eighteenth and nineteenth centuries.

Whether expressed in the domain of education, government, culture, or imperial/colonial conquest, the idea of civilization relies on a belief in a (real or potential) human condition of "being civil" that is opposed to a (real or potential) human condition of "being savage."

The violence inherent in such a splitting of human possibilities is related to the violence that results from efforts to "civilize" ourselves and others, and from our own violent reactions to such efforts.

2.

Complex questions about civilization require that we examine not merely physical violence, physical health, and physical security, but hidden violence, psychic unhealth, and ontological insecurity.

One way to do so is to define "civilization" as the conversion of physical violence and overt domination into structural, invisible, and internalized violence and self-violence.

Many thoughtful critics of modernity, from Karl Marx to Friedrich Nietzsche to Sigmund Freud to Michel Foucault, have expounded this thesis, yet one of its most memorable depictions remains Kafka's "A Report to an Academy," in which the main character, Rotpeter the ape, describes his miraculous transformation into a human being, thus:

> I learned things, gentlemen. Ah, one learns things when one has to; one learns when one needs a way out; one learns at all costs. One stands over oneself with a whip; one flays oneself at the slightest opposition. (1971, 258)

The self-violence at the heart of Rotpeter's project of self-civilization, and the analogy drawn between the training of an ape, the education of a child, and the assimilation of a creature into human culture and civilization, all suggest a fruitful line of questioning:

What does it really mean to be civil?

And what types of violence are most destructive to civil being?

Here, we must approach "civil being" as something much more meaningful than mere "politeness." Rather, civil being includes that central norm of inter-subjective ethics and the governing principle of object-relations: "Being civil" depends, first, on an individual's being, and, second, on his or her ability to treat others as separate beings, which entails preserving boundaries and relating with others across those boundaries in authentic and meaningful ways.

3.

Rotpeter the ape discovers, in captivity and amidst torture and terror, that he is able to mimic the behavior, speech, and thought of the humans who have imprisoned him, but, like many of Kafka's characters, Rotpeter lacks the ability to be, to act, and to relate civilly.

Rotpeter's identification with his captors is the *only* "way out" of his cage (253), but it is also *only* a "way out": nothing more.

His civilization is coerced assimilation: a process by which he repudiates in himself all that is not identical to those around him. Having internalized the demands of his tormentors, Rotpeter ultimately thanks his "teachers" for helping him to break his authentic nature, for "fighting on the same side against the nature of apes" (257).

Rotpeter's civilizers train him to smoke a pipe and drink schnapps, but they do not help him develop a self that is capable of being on its own, or of interacting with others in meaningful ways.

Indeed, Rotpeter is like a human but incapable of being human, for he is incapable of acting spontaneously in the world, or of communicating with others, or of challenging the world around him without fearing a return to his dreadful cage. That his "civilization" was founded upon fear, pain, torment, and imprisonment means that the specter of these horrors haunts his thoughts and deeds, keeping him "human" in a superficial sense but undermining any true humanity he might achieve.

In the end, Rotpeter feels compelled to cover up even his own story of transformation by declaring that his words contain no communicative content, no emotion, no meaning: "I am only imparting knowledge, I am only making a report. To you, also, honored Members of the Academy, I have only made a report" (259).

Rotpeter's missed, failed, or empty civilization thus asks us to reflect upon the fear, pain, and torment motivating our own.

If civilizing practices, such as child-rearing, education, and more, are carried out by those who, themselves, fear a cage — a cage of failure, a cage of shame, a cage of depression — then these practices *cannot* facilitate the development of autonomous, authentic human beings.

If we must be civilized *or else,* then our eventual identification with our "civilizers" (and with their violence and self-violence) will be all that protects us from experiencing ourselves as "savage," abhorrent, worthless.

4.

The violence, therefore, that informs the split between "civilized" and "savage" is transmitted via civilizing individuals, families, groups, organizations, and institutions, and is unleashed upon the "uncivilized" aspects of ourselves and others in the name of progress.

This aspect of our civilization is too often ignored and defended by our manic, if not compulsive, attention to visible signs of "progress" in civilization: technological change, economic growth, physical or material change, and the like.

To the extent that our civilizing practices depend upon shared (self-)hatred of the uncivilized, they make *civil being* impossible, not only because they undercut an individual's authentic being — which must learn to tolerate and integrate the uncivilized aspects of the self — but because individuals who are civilized in this way cannot relate with others who do *not* hate themselves.

That is, persons civilized in such a way can only identify with those who hate their selves. Those who do not hate their selves are suspected to be outsiders, strangers, naïvely "sovereign subjects," dangerous individuals.

Der Hund ist los: Kafka's Mysterious Investigations

I.

In German, *"Was ist los?"* [literally: "What is loose?"] is a greeting, akin to, "What's going on?" but with a slightly negative connotation, as in, "What is the matter?"

Every German-speaking person has likely heard the reply, *"Der Hund ist los"* [literally: "The dog is loose"], or some variation thereof: *"Der Hund ist los and und die Katze ist in der Keller"* ["The dog is loose and the cat is in the cellar"].

A greeting in the form of a question is here met not with an answer but with reply, a reply that is a joke, and a joke that is, frankly, a bad joke.

If it is difficult to imagine anything valuable arising from such trivialities, consider the fact that "What is loose?" also suggests, ""What is lost?" to which a jocular reply, while communicating little in manifest content, may express the need to deflect the question.

On the other hand, if one were to ask a dog, *"Was ist los?"* and the dog were to respond, *"Der Hund ist los,"* the question would have found a substantial, and agonizing, answer.

2.

In Kafka's difficult story, *"Forschungen eines Hundes"* ["Investigations of a Dog"], the eponymous yet unnamed narrator (who is a dog, himself) tells us that all dogs "live together in a literal heap," that "nothing can prevent us from satisfying that communal impulse," and that "all our laws and institutions [...] go back to this longing for the greatest bliss we are capable of, the warm comfort of being together" (1971, 279).

Thus, when, in his youth, our dog spies seven dogs who dance, stand on their hind legs ("uncovering their nakedness"), and make an incredible music without voices—thereby suggesting that "Nature were an error" (284)—he objects to their seemingly willful violation of both the letter and the spirit of dog law.

He demands to know what they are doing. (Perhaps he might have asked them, *"Was ist los!?"*)

But, to his question, "they—incredible! incredible! They never replied, behaved, as if [he] were not there" (283).

Replying to other dogs is "unconditionally command[ed]" by dog law, so their failure to reply is yet another offense against the law that all dogs behave in such a way as to affirm every dog's membership in "the canine community" (278).

Our dog's attempts to question the seven dogs, perhaps even to correct them, are in vain, for the seven dogs reply only by continuing their obscenities.

They make a mockery of dogdom, even though they do not do so joyfully. Instead, it seemed as if they danced and made music under compulsion, "quiver[ing] at every step with a perpetual apprehension, as if rigid with despair" (283).

Our dog admits that it is possible that he was deluded, confused, or mistaken in his vision: that he witnessed no such event. But he is not deterred by doubt from his subsequent investigations.

Instead, this "concert" becomes the foundation of his inquiries into the mysteries of dog existence.

He begins, like an adolescent might, by making "accusations and investigations," trying "to drag others to the place where all this had happened [...] to show everybody where I had stood and the seven had stood, and where and how they had danced and made their music" (285).

These activities, he later admits, "robbed me of a great part of my childhood" (286) and inaugurated his ill-fated study, for which — he reminds the reader several times — he is inadequate, unprepared by formal training.

So, our dog turns his attention to a different but not unrelated subject: the greatest mystery of dogdom, upon which countless essays have been published and circulated among the dog community: the question of "what the canine race nourishe[s] itself upon."

The answer to this question is given to every dog in infancy in the form of a single imperative to "water the ground as much as you can," for it is well known that the watering of the ground, in addition to the performance of "certain spells, songs, and ritual movements" procures dogs' nourishment from the earth (286–87).

But if one inquires further, if one asks, for example, "But where does the earth procure the food which it gives to dogs," no answer can or will be given.

To ask such a question is to elicit only a reply, such as, "If you haven't enough to eat, we'll give you some of ours," which is not only untrue, since dogs are not known for sharing food, but tangential at best, to the matter at hand.

For our dog, such a response is not even a reply but a bad joke, a "jest," a form of "raillery" (288), not unlike, *"Der Hund ist los."*

This sort of jest is but one way in which our dog feels that other dogs seek to divert him from his quest. If other dogs have occasionally shared their food with him, it was merely in order to shut him up.

3.

While, at first, our dog was certain that others were attempting to seduce him into complacency, eventually, he hit upon an insight into his own activity. "I was the one," he confesses, "who was trying to seduce the others, and [...] I was actually successful up to a certain point," for

> only with the assistance of the whole dog world could I begin to understand my own questions. [...] It is not merely flesh and blood that we have in common, but knowledge also, and not only knowledge, but the key to it as well. I do not possess that except in common with all the others; I cannot grasp it without their help. The hardest bones, containing the richest marrow, can be conquered only by a united crunching of the teeth of all dogs. (289–91)

Indeed, our dog admits that all along he has wanted to use the dog community to help him gather knowledge, which he would hoard greedily, although it would ultimately sicken him:

> I want to compel all dogs thus to assemble together, I want the bones to crack open under the pressure of their collective preparedness, and then I want to dismiss them to the ordinary life that they love, while all by myself, quite alone, I lap up the marrow. That sounds monstrous, almost as if I wanted to feed on the marrow, not merely of a bone, but of the whole canine race itself. But it is only a metaphor. The marrow that I am discussing here is no food; on the contrary, it is a poison. (291)

So, our dog needs the dog community to find answers to his questions, questions which the dog community does not, itself, seem capable of answering and which, we may surmise, should they be answered, would spell the end of "the ordinary life" of dogs.

Our dog, then, wishes to be alone in drinking the marrow of knowledge, which is also a poison: the poison that will kill the dog (and/or the doggishness, and/or the doggedness) within him.

He acknowledges that his "questions only serve as a goad to myself; I only want to be stimulated by the silence which rises up around me as the ultimate answer. How long will you be able to endure the fact that the world of dogs [...] is pledged to silence and always will be?" (291).

And yet he too is a "bulwark of silence." He, too, has "the impulse to question and the impulse not to answer" (293). Thus, "all this ceaseless labor — to what end? Merely to entomb oneself deeper and deeper in silence, it seems, so deep that one can never be dragged out of it again by anybody" (299).

4.

It is hard not to remark the resemblances between the shocking concert our dog witnesses and a kind of traumatizing, Freudian "primal scene," just as it is hard to ignore the themes of food, hunger, and fasting that run throughout the story. But none of these themes brings us much closer to understanding the story's meaning. Worse, they may be distractions.

The extensive literary commentary on the story — rife with discussions of sex and food (see, e.g., Williams 2007) — may only demonstrate that we cannot help ourselves but to return and return, to be both bored and fascinated, like dogs, by these subjects.

It is true that our dog undertakes a lengthy fast as an experiment to discover the source of dogs' nourishment. And it is true that fasting is contrary to the laws of dogdom as well as to the most fundamental of a dog's instincts.

But what our dog is after is an ultimate understanding that he cannot conceive. The inconceivable, then, is the real foundation of his inquiries. Put another way, he is motivated by and fascinated by that which he cannot imagine.

Primal scenes of singing dogs and lengthy fasts unto delirium are but stand-ins, as it were, for the impossible understanding he wishes to possess.

5.

Here, then, are the real conundrums:

Our dog hates silence, but admits that silence is his ultimate goal.

The dog community is pledged to silence, and yet they are forbidden to be silent.

In fact, the dog community constantly asks questions, and constantly replies to each other's greetings, but only to drown out and "obliterate the trace of genuine questions" (297).

Dogs are naturally groupish, drawn to live together, and even our dog admits that his goal, much of the time, is easily achieved with a howl or a bite: "amiable attention, friendly contiguity, honest acceptance, ardent embraces, barks that mingle as one: everything is directed toward achieving an ecstasy, a forgetting and finding again" (290). And yet the seven dogs are different, and witnessing their difference marks our dog as different, separate, exiled.

These (apparent) contradictions suggest that we ask: What does our dog mean by "a forgetting and a finding again"?

Does he mean that to ask impossible questions is to seek not *answers* but *replies,* a series of replies, even an assurance of never-ending replies?

A reply is not as satisfying as an answer, but a reply may be given again and again, whereas an answer, presumably, need be given only once.

Consider, on this point, the chatter of Vladimir and Estragon in Samuel Beckett's *Waiting for Godot* (1956). The often comic, often tragic absurdity of their speech, its madness even, may be applied according to a certain method: It assures endless, although confounding, conversation.

It ensures contact and togetherness, but not communication and relatedness. Indeed, it assures the absence and poverty of communication, for fear that genuine communication and relatedness might destroy the security of a more primitive contact and togetherness.

Or consider the case of Job, who receives, at best, a tangential reply, but not an answer, to his interrogations of God. God speaks to Job out of the whirlwind with no real regard for Job's inquiries, complaints, and protestations. God declares His supreme majesty and power. He overwhelms Job in His reply.

It is difficult to know whether Job is satisfied by this. Perhaps God's reply resounds in Job's ears until the day Job dies. Perhaps this continued "presence" of God — even a different and diminished God — is better, in some sense, than an answer to the question: "Why did the God Job thought he knew betray Job, permitting all that Job loved to be destroyed?"

What if mysteries exist so that we always have something about which to cry out, as if we were seeking answers when, in fact, we seek only endless and repetitive (and perhaps even insubstantial or boring or meaningless) replies?

What if, even more than we need answers, we need replies to assure us that we are not alone in silence?

What if silence, itself, is not categorically distinct from a reply but is, in essence, a reply that carries a kind of meaning? It is, after all, in a kind of silence that we, as children, first encounter the idea: "not good enough," i.e., "I am not good enough to deserve the response from the other that I most desire."

What if it is, then, upon the reply that is contained in silence that we construct a psychic shrine to missing words, missing touches, missing persons, and other mysteries: an invisible temple, and a poor substitute for a home.

6.

Our dog (ambivalently) wishes to be alone, and is encouraged in this quest by at least three examples of dogs who have achieved a definitive separation from the canine community: (1) the seven dog musicians, (2) the "soaring dogs" (294), who have never been seen but of whom many credible accounts have been given, and (3) the ancient or original dogs.

Soaring dogs are, to our dog, an outrage, for they are very small and let their legs "fall into desuetude." Worse, they "reap without having sowed," since they do not "water the ground" or contribute to the collective life of dogs in any way but still gather nourishment from the earth, only to return to their "senseless occupation" of floating in the air (294).

Since they are literally set above other dogs, they are imagined to hold a "higher" knowledge and, indeed, "are perpetually talking, partly of their philosophical reflections, with which [...] they can continuously occupy themselves, partly of the observations they have made form their exalted stations" (295). But their philosophies are worthless and, according to our dog, in reality, contribute nothing to dogdom.

The ancient or original dogs, about whom we can only conjecture, brought the dog community together but, in doing so, lost "the Word" and condemned all dogs to an ignorance and a silence about that which was most sacred.

No one knows, of course, what "the Word" is or was, but it is imagined by our dog not to be a set of laws but as a divine presence, much as John (1:1–2, KJV) famously begins his gospel: "In the beginning was the Word, and the Word was with God, and the Word was God. The same was in the beginning with God."

Their fates less determined by habit, custom, and community life, the early generations of dogs had the opportunity to seize upon "the Word" but failed. "The edifice of dogdom was still loosely put together, the true Word could still have intervened, planning or replanning the structure, changing it at will, transforming it into its opposite," just as "the Word was there, was very near at least, on the tip of everyone's tongue, anyone might have hit upon it" (Kafka 1971, 300).

In the beginning, the ancient dogs were closer to "the Word." It was therefore "easier to get them to speak out," "even if nobody actually succeeded in doing that" (299), but the ancients "strayed" (got lost, got loose [*los*]), not knowing their "their aberration was to be an endless one" (300), and began to enjoy "dog life," which is a life without the possibility of uttering or hearing the true Word, without the possibility of answering the ultimate questions.

The ancient dogs committed the canine version of original sin. They left behind that which was divine in order to become "doggish" (300), to enjoy ordinary life.

Now, the Word is lost and can never be found. This is not the fault of the current, "fallen" generation of dogs. For them, the Word is but "the thousandth forgetting of a dream forgotten one thousand times" (300), which is why it is possible to say that a dream forgotten a thousand times has an exquisite quality.

7.

In this story, then, we are presented with at least two kinds of silence and at least two kinds of guilt.

There is, first, the silence of the ancient dogs, who strayed from "the Word," but who could have run back to it, "hounded" it, chased after it "doggedly," and perhaps even have heard or spoken it.

But there is also the silence of latter-day dogs, locked in ignorance, fated never to know "the true Word," although impelled by dog nature to investigate and question.

Since the potential to discover "the Word" is lost today, silence is what holds dogs together in their community. The communal bonds of dogs are forged in silence. Even questions, even replies, even the loudest barking of dogs are parts of this silence: a reminder that, while words or barks may be uttered, "the Word" shall never again be spoken or heard.

In the same way, the original guilt of the original dogs, who condemned all future dogs to a life of ordinary communality but severance from the divine, is a (poisoned) gift to latter-day dogs, who now hasten "in almost guiltless silence toward death in a world darkened by others" (300).

Of course, should a dog attempt to reject his fate, his instinct, and, with apologies to Marx, his "species-being," the guilt the dog experiences only brings him closer to the community of dogs and their eternal silence, which is, after all, what our dog truly seeks.

Perhaps the dream of no longer being a dog is shared by all dogs, even the most contented, ordinary dog.

Perhaps this dream is dreamt a thousand times or more, perhaps every time a dog sleeps. But this dream, like the Word — and which may very well be "the Word," itself — is never remembered, always forgotten.

W.R. Bion suggests that, in our nascent states, we encounter proscriptions against seeking "the Word," the ultimate truth, mainly from "Arf Arfer" [i.e., "Our Father Who Art in Heaven"] (Bion 1982; Grotstein 2007, 229).

But, of course, "the Word" is merely imagined, just as "Arf Arfer" is imagined.

Both "the Word" and "Arf Arfer" are imagined and then imagined to have been lost.

In guilt, we imagine them, then we imagine that we have abandoned "Arf Arfer" and His Word, or that they have abandoned us, which, psychologically, amounts to the same thing, since if we imagine to have been abandoned, we find ways to justify our abandonment by imagining that we deserved to be abandoned.

In any case, we imagine that we cannot know "the Word" and that we are simultaneously condemned for our ignorance of it.

Then, in our frustration and anxiety, we declare "the Word" to be a mystery, which, at least, is something that can be worshipped in place of the absence of the Word and the divinity who held it.

Of course, this worship of the mystery that arises from the imagined loss of an imagined Word uttered by an imagined divinity takes place in silence.

The irresolubility of the mystery is attributed to our inheritance of "instinct," the "more profound cause of [our] scientific incapacity" (Kafka 1971, 315–16), but is, actually, the most basic necessity of this form of communal, religious practice.

Finally, we imagine our "instinct not to know" to be our hereditary sin, leaving an indelible mark upon our identity.

We are guilty of the "sin of wanting to know" that which cannot and ought not be known (Camus 1955, 49).

Since we cannot be rid of our hereditary sin, all we can do is torment ourselves with endless investigations conducted in such a way as to be — necessarily — fruitless.

A Simple Heart, Father, and Flaubert

1.

Once my father could no longer walk the dogs and feed the ducks, the life rushed out of him as if it had been exorcized.

Even the cancer doctors were flabbergasted.

One day, he was scheduled for surgery. The next day, talk of hospices. The next day, he was sent home to die.

I flew to Texas to say goodbye.

2.

He lay on a couch in the living room and we held hands through his delirium.

He spent four hours alternating between sleep and confused consternation over whether — and, if so, how — to sit up.

When he rose, his wife and I held him up like Jesus, and helped him urinate into a garbage can.

The only lucid gesture he made was out of character and not in jest. I asked him how he was feeling and he raised up his head, held his index finger to his temple like a gun, and made a child's gunshot noise: "Pkkkkkew!"

He was not religious, but his wife insisted that, if their ashes were to be conjoined upon her death, he had to find belief. So he spent his final days receiving visits from a priest, trying to convince himself that God was real.

Even this coerced, death-bed conversion seemed to give him some comfort: He could pretend to believe he'd not be alone in a jar of ash for all eternity.

3.

As a young child, age four or five, I walked with my father through Union Station in Chicago, Illinois.

A young woman rapidly approached us and fastened an "I ♥ Chicago" pin on my shirt. Then she demanded a dollar from my father, to pay for the pin.

My father was horrified. He looked at me, of all people, for guidance. He panicked.

He dropped his briefcase with a startle as the woman effectively patted him down.

When he finally turned out his pockets, a thousand pennies burst forth: a torrent of rusted blood, as if he'd hit an artery.

The pennies made a sound like shattering glass, one of the worst I've heard.

My father went white, unable to stop the hemorrhage, as the pennies rolled in all directions across the station's marble floors.

Then, in his charcoal business suit, he got on his hands and knees to pick them up, while the woman and I stood motionless, in silence.

I hated the woman and was ashamed of my father for reasons I could not understand.

Worse, I felt sick because the situation was at least partly predicated on my father's sincere but incorrect belief that I was interested in a worthless pin, foisted upon me indecently, which, since then, had been slowly tearing a hole in my threadbare t-shirt.

(The other driver of the situation was my father's discomfort with conflict and with mobilizing aggression, even when necessary.)

How could I be interested in such a thing, a thing given in such a way, not even "given" so much as "extorted" from my father, who was so humble that he would rather crawl across a filthy floor than deny his son the merest trinket, a trinket whose interest was null but whose interest could never be explored because to discuss it would have been somehow akin to crawling across a filthy floor all over again? Was I a worthless thing for accepting the pin? Would pretending to cherish it make me worthless? Was my father worthless, bested by a rudimentary grift?

The four-or-five-year-old versions of these thoughts tore through my head with the noise of a thousand pennies and the violence of metal ripping through a child's t-shirt.

I watched my father gather up his change, count a dollar's worth, pay the woman, collect himself, and heave a sigh. I think I said, "Thanks, Dad."

4.

Over the years, when I visited my father — which typically included a day of air travel, a rental car, an hours-long drive, and a stop at the grocery store for supplies — I would arrive to his absence.

He would immediately leave to smoke, or run an errand, or go to the bathroom, or feed the ducks, as if he were overwhelmed by the prospect of greeting me.

It is terrible to consider what I must have been to him: a source of discomfort, anxiety, misinterest, fear.

I don't recall that he ever asked me a question about myself or my life. He did not know any details about me, where I worked, what I did. He did not keep my address or telephone number.

Since talking was out of the question, eventually we hit upon doing activities together, while trying to relate, so we'd have quick access to a distraction from our surprising lack of relationship. For the last twenty years of his life, we played pool, exchanging three-word utterances in between shots or talk of shots.

My father played for hours every night. He studied the game obsessively. He ran leagues and tournaments anywhere he could: run-down pool halls and motorcycle bars. He gave money to the people he met. He let them stay at his house if they were fighting with a boyfriend, girlfriend, husband, wife, or roommate. They used him for money. He bought one a used car he could hardly afford, which angered me for several reasons, not least because I was drowning in debt in graduate school, considering bankruptcy, working three jobs, and living without reliable transportation or health insurance.

He never imagined I could be in need or pain. Eventually, I found myself going out of the way to tell him stories of travail, injury, sickness, tragedy, loss. He could not hear them. All he could say, between manic movements and yelling at the dogs and checking his watch, was, "Welp, you seem fine."

One might say: This is a father who believes in his son.

One might say, with greater precision: This is a father who knows his son in a certain way, who wishes to know an invulnerable, almost omnipotent, son. The fantasy of this son is threatened by the real son's life, which must never be explored.

In any case, with respect to the game of pool, I should have been no match for him, but when I visited, I won, or he lost, even if I ceased to try, perhaps because, to him, I was invulnerable and omnipotent, or had to be. This phenomenon, which we were both forced to acknowledge, devastated him.

Typically, when he became adequately unnerved, he would encourage me to go to the bar and drink a beer, so he could practice.

So there I would sit, at a strange, suburban bar, watching my father shoot the same shot one hundred times, as he had done for years, talking to the billiard balls so easily, so comfortably, without any sign of tension.

5.

As a child, when I got sad or scared, I was told to "just ignore it" or else, Dad said, "the boy in Cincinnati" would be happy.

It was with a kind of *contrapasso,* both more stark and less imaginative than Dante's, that he understood the moral world: zero-sum, like a child or a Fundamentalist.

This boy in Cincinnati, whom I had never met, was my enemy, and when I was happy, Dad said, the boy in Cincinnati was sad.

When the boy in Cincinnati was loved, I was hated.

When I erred, the boy in Cincinnati was rewarded.

Sometimes the boy in Cincinnati must have felt good, at which point Mom would spank me and tell me she knew everything inside of me, until I went to pieces.

Dad did not approve of spanking, nor of discussions of what was inside of me, but was unable to intervene because such activities could not be comprehended by the simple scale that was Cincinnati justice.

6.

You could not have paid my father to read Flaubert, but if he had, he would have liked Félicité, the heroine of one of Flaubert's best short works, the first of his *Trois Contes*: *"Un Cœur Simple"* ["A Simple Heart"].

"Simple" can mean many things: guilelessness, innocence, naturalness, and purity, but also provinciality, poverty, primitivism, and ignorance.

Both father and Félicité had honorable instincts, worked tirelessly to provide for their families, economized, and served others in their way.

Father religiously fed, sheltered, and likely damaged the long-term health of flocks of suburban ducks until he died. Félicité died in communion with her dead, stuffed parrot Loulou, in whose image she saw the Holy Ghost.

At the first communion of her charge, Virginie, Félicité nearly fainted with joy. At our suburban church, my father stood silently during the weekly collective confession because he felt that he had not committed the (abstract) sins to which the congregation was collectively confessing.

If we believe Showalter (1966), and see "A Simple Heart" as a kind of reply to Bernardin de Saint-Pierre, we find the names of the Aubain children in Bernardin's story "Paul et Virginie." Bernardin took a teenaged wife when he was in his fifties. She served as something of a domestic maid to him and bore him two children, Paul and Virginie, before dying of tuberculosis. Her name was Félicité.

Flaubert and Bernardin corresponded only once or twice, but there is a central motif in Bernardin's *La chaumière indienne* [*The Indian Hut*] (1895, 285–89) that may shed light on the meaning of "A Simple Heart."

An academic and a pariah discuss how to find truth and happiness. The academic asks:

> "With what sense or faculty shall we look for the truth, since the mind or the intelligence is not capable of finding it." And the pariah says: "With a simple heart. The senses and the mind can be mistaken, but a simple heart can never be mistaken. A simple heart has never pretended to hear what it has not heard, nor pretended to believe what it does not believe. Even nature, if we consider it with a simple heart, we will be able to see God in it. We must search for the truth with a simple heart."

But the tragedy of a simple heart, is that a simple heart is not enough to live an adult life, a life of interest.

My father was, I fear, too simple to find interest in his adult life, or in the lives of others, even in the lives of his children.

Yet, he was too complex to enjoy the source of Félicité's felicity: that, as Showalter aptly remarks, she is so simple, ignorant, and submissive that "she can overlook a fact the rest of us cannot escape: that she deserves a better fate" (1966, 55).

A Dream of Success

I'm sitting on the wooden floor of a cloistered, patchwork monastery cut into the side of a mountain, awaiting the arrival of a grey-bearded man who is not my father but who is, nonetheless, not unfatherly.

The enormous, ancient doors, covered with gold rings, will soon part to expose the dark, silent interior to fierce sunlight and terrible wind.

I both dread and eagerly anticipate this moment.

When the doors finally open and the fatherly man, barely visible, looms silently, I am overwhelmed by a violent sickness that rushes through my gut.

I begin to sob.

I feel around the floor and find a sharp rock, which I instinctively hurl at the man, and yet I also want him, need him, to enter, as his willingness to join me signifies something about my worth.

The man enters and I know instantly that I have succeeded, that I am saved, saved from myself, made good.

But I also know that this salvation comes at a grave cost because, in exchange for such grace, I must forsake an element of myself, something I have never truly encountered but that I nevertheless hold dear, or that I ought to hold dear, or that I ought to have held dear.

I must physically expel from my body this element and roll it out the doors and down the mountainside into the valley, where the snow and ice will quickly bury it and where, after the thaw, wolves will devour it.

In response to this exchange and my anxiety about it, my body collapses into a fleshy liquid and forms a sort of puddle, much of which remains upon the monastery's floor, but some of which manages to ooze beneath the great doors and to slide down and down, to its quiet fate.

Voir Dire

1.

Voir dire does not mean what the New York State government thinks it means.

When, finally, I had to submit myself for jury duty, everyone was made to watch a video starring actors from the television series, *Law and Order.*

It started, without warning, on each TV of a four-TV cluster bolted to the ceiling of an awful, underground waiting room. The video was incredibly loud. It commanded attention.

"There's no escape!" I said out loud, and looked to others near me for a smile or nod or some form of confirmation, finding none.

What I wanted to say, but refrained from saying, was that the four-TV cluster—broadcasting itself to all points of the compass—is a sort of inverted panopticon that transforms even contemporary waiting areas into prison houses (see Bentham 1791).

2.

The (conscious) aim of the video was to offer viewers an introduction to the history and nature of judicial processes.

I had the powerful sense while watching it that I was being put on, not least because it reduced the entirety of legal history to three (Western) epochs and still managed to caricature them terribly.

First, there was ancient Rome, where trials were dominated by the authority of judges (*boo!*).

Then, there were the "middle ages," in which no legal procedure existed except the trial by ordeal: mobs of dirty townsfolk tormenting accused persons, to full Monty Pythonesque effect (*boo!*).

Finally, there was the modern American legal system, paragon of reason and rectitude *(yay!)*.

Voir dire, the video went on to say, came from the French verbs, *voir,* meaning to see, and *dire,* meaning to say.

So, *voir dire,* the blaring video announced, meant to see what prospective jurors will say.

"That's wrong!" I said out loud, again half-hoping for some kind of acknowledgment, and again finding none.

This obvious lack of empathetic, emotional, or intellectual relatedness between me and my comrades added to the self-hatred and disgust I was already feeling.

You see, I was fairly revolted at myself because, of a large, fairly random sample of citizens of Buffalo, NY—or even, one might say, of a sample skewed toward those without the wherewithal to evade jury duty—I was *the only one* to show up substantially late.

If there were statistical significance to this datum, it would demonstrate that my life, my discipline, and my self were all less "together" than everyone else's.

3.

In any case, the French would be the old French *voir(e),* with a Latin root of *verum* [truth], because the point is not just to see whatever crap spills out of jurors' mouths—I slipped into several vulgarities that day—but to have them speak the goddamned (*maudit*) truth.

4.

Once we were called into the courtroom, the judge pulled eleven of us up into the jury box at a time, while the rest waited in the gallery: the rows, like pews, that hold the court's audience.

When the District Attorney—"Must be an important case," I thought, this time keeping my thoughts to myself—asked everyone's profession and discovered I was a professor, he instantly looked worried, became condescending, and treated me like a dangerous fool. It was enraging to hear him speak.

He asked me, condescendingly, "*Can* you understand that there may be variability in witness accounts and interpretations of events? And *can* you understand that that this doesn't mean you should just throw out everything everyone says?"

"Yes," I replied, wishing to say, "*Can* you meet me outside so I can beat the shit out of you?"

"Because," he continued, "sometimes people like yourself, doctors and such, like to see things clearly, in black and white, true and false."

"Uh huh," I muttered, wishing to say, "You could not be more stupid or wrong, you fucking pompous dolt."

5.

Later, he asked if anyone had been charged with a crime, and, if so, to raise your hand, explain the charge, and say a few words about how the experience "might affect you as a juror."

One man said he had been charged with domestic violence. When asked what the result of the charges were, the man muttered, "anger management," angrily.

When pressed by the judge to say whether he had been "convicted" or "acquitted," the man, who clearly never understood these words nor their implications for his own legal status, merely said that "it makes him real angry" that, when he tells people he's been charged with domestic violence, "everyone assumes it was physical violence," that he beat his wife.

Instead, he insisted, "not all violence is physical."

His was "mental."

It was "mental violence."

And — we could rest assured — it would not affect his ability to administer justice at all.

6.

District Attorney: "Has anyone else ever been charged or convicted of a crime?"

Juror #10 (Me): "Including misdemeanors?"

District Attorney: "Yes."

Juror #10 (Me): "I pled no contest to jumping a subway turnstile in Manhattan in 1992."

District Attorney, Judge, seated jury pool, and audience: [Loud laughter]

District Attorney: "Okay [continued laughter]. Can everyone seated promise to be impartial and to leave all personal sympathies, beliefs, and emotions behind?

Juror #10 (Me): "I am sorry to be picky here but I am getting confused about the extent to which you want to hear about our beliefs. For instance, I have certain beliefs about the police, about incarceration, and about the judicial system. Do you want us to disclose these things that might make impartiality difficult for us, which is not to say impossible — and even this would only be possible to the extent that we are conscious of them — or do you want us to say whether we think we can be impartial in spite of what beliefs or biases we may have?"

Judge [dismissively]: "That question is way too complicated."

District Attorney, Judge, seated jury pool, and audience: [Loud laughter]

Me: "Okay."

District Attorney, Judge, seated jury pool, and audience: [Mild laughter]

[Ninety minutes later]

Judge: "Juror #10 is dismissed."

How To Be a Victim: Camus's Plagues and Poisons

I.

In 1947, Gallimard published Algerian-French writer Albert Camus's allegorical novel, *La peste* [*The Plague*]. It would become an important part of Camus's candidacy for the Nobel Prize in Literature, awarded to him in 1957. While many scholars feel that *The Plague* is not Camus's best work, its worldwide popularity has made it one of the best-known works of art concerning plagues, rivaling Boccaccio's *Decameron,* Daniel Dafoe's *A Journal of the Plague Year,* and Ingmar Bergman's film, *The Seventh Seal.*

In Camus's *The Plague,* a mysterious disease suddenly strikes the town of Oran, whose borders are quickly closed and many of whose residents quickly become ill and die. Through the voices of his protagonists, Dr. Bernard Rieux and journalist-turned-activist Jean Tarrou, Camus shakes his fist at the plague, at the world, at God, and at all who are not adequately outraged, asking how such misery could ever be justified.

But Camus's novel is not really about a plague. Written in the aftermath of the Second World War, the plague it describes is an allegory for the war, for Nazi atrocities, and for other forms of terror.

What is more, *The Plague* is ultimately concerned not with either a bacillus or a war, but with our moral stance against them. The plague, itself, is a prop for the ethical and existential dilemmas raised by the reality of human suffering and the problem of choosing how and when to fight, whom to spare, and whom to cast aside.

The Plague asks: How should we live in a time of terror? Are we permitted to love and to be happy, or must we sacrifice our personal projects for the sake of combatting suffering? Are we permitted to flee, either in body or in mind? And how can we avoid the attitude of Cottard, who embraces the plague as a great equalizer, a crisis that eclipses his crimes and fears?

Camus never answers these questions directly, of course. But his characters and their (often heavy-handed) monologues give us ample clues as to his thoughts. Camus was concerned primarily with what we might call "moral plague": not with the fact that some people will inevitably die untimely deaths due to disease, neglect, war, crime, poverty, and the like, but with the likelihood that the rest of us will find ways to rationalize this suffering and these deaths.

That our acceptance of the reality of "plague" made us carriers of "plague" was Camus's greatest concern, and, perhaps, his least convincing moral-philosophical line of argument.

2.

In *The Plague,* Dr. Bernard Rieux leaves his ailing wife in a sanitarium outside the city, while he remains in the town of Oran, tirelessly fighting the plague. Dr. Rieux knows that his efforts are largely futile, for the plague will run its course and take its toll.

He also knows that he must become a partly oppressive solution to the largely oppressive problem of the epidemic. Dr. Rieux must scan citizens for symptoms, must separate ill from well members of families, and must send the infected to makeshift hospitals that resemble concentration camps. He must sacrifice some for the good of others. He and his workers do not even discuss taking their services into the Arab Quarter, whose residents are ravaged by pestilence and are all but annihilated.

Much of Rieux's personality is effaced by his work. He loses something profound within himself: his vital spirit or his creative spark, perhaps. One wonders whether this loss permits him to do his job so effectively, to separate and quarantine, to condemn and to heal.

Camus's *Plague* seeks to remind us that it is when we forget our inevitable susceptibility to "carrying" moral plagues that we become agents and transmitters ourselves. That is, especially in times of plague, we must be vigilantly on guard against our own temptation to seek solace in nihilism, neutrality, indifference, or moral absolutism.

3.

Of course, a part of us longs for plagues, depends on them. Plagues are exciting. Plagues relieve us of daily stresses. Hysterical media coverage and conversations about the terror of the month (from ebola to avian flu to dirty bombs to mass shootings to neo-Nazi rallies) ought to make us aware of the part of us that relishes disaster or the possibility of disaster.

Plagues also offer us the opportunity to feel innocent. The more evil the plague, the more gruesome the terror, the more innocent we feel in voicing our condemnation or opposition.

Plagues, in this sense, become necessary evils, necessary primarily for the maintenance of certain psychological states that have become increasingly common: the state of perennial wariness and victimhood, identification with the oppressed, and the mentality of a survivalist.

We depend upon plagues to give our quest for survival the moral standing we feel it deserves.

Unfortunately, the state of mind that is best suited for surviving plagues, while it may seem attractive when a group of attractive TV characters pull together to slaughter zombies or vampires, is *not* a state of mind that is particularly conducive to doing the difficult, often tedious work of being, doing, and relating as whole, active persons in highly complex, political, civil, and interpersonal environments, where problems are not as simple as life or death, good or evil, plague or cure.

When each decision is framed as a matter of survival, when the government itself is presented as an entity that can either save or destroy us, when our popular discourse skips from crisis to crisis, perhaps hoping each time that in vanquishing the present enemy we will vanquish them all, then we know we are not merely in a state of crisis, but in a state of *dependency* upon crisis.

4.

Contra Camus, it does not help to shake our fist at the world, at humanity, at the government, or at God, asking for an authority to justify or rectify what has been done.

The real "moral plague" that confronts us is one in which we are tempted to lurch from tragedy to tragedy, feeling all the while that there isn't much a person can do — and perhaps there isn't — to fight the seemingly unending succession of evils.

We dread becoming identified with victimizers and plague agents, so we decide we must become victims and change agents. We defend against our impotence by indulging in fantasies of omnipotence. We may even create or amplify crises, hoping that, in the new crises, our feelings of helplessness and irrelevance will be replaced with the feeling of aliveness and activity.

Here we must call upon a rudimentary distinction between, on one hand, change as an activity in which things — the self, the group, an institution, a policy, et cetera — are made new or different from what they were, and, on the other hand, change as a component of group identity and a fantasy of omnipotence.

5.

Consider the late Elie Wiesel, who remarked in his 1986 Nobel Peace Prize acceptance speech: "We must always take sides. Neutrality helps the oppressor, never the victim. Silence encourages the tormentor, never the tormented. [...] Wherever men or women are persecuted because of their race, religion, or political views, that place must—at that moment—become the center of the universe" (quoted in Reilly 2016).

There are at least two remarkable things about this passage. The first is the way that an odd idea—that neutrality is never neutral—is presented as an obvious truth, in no need of explanation or evidence. That this argument is presented in this way tells us something about its psychic meaning: that it is not really intended to be a philosophical claim about neutrality, nor an empirical claim about politics or history.

Instead, the statement expresses an identification with a group, a group for whom the words spoken require no evidence because they are already known and are, therefore, self-evident. While this group may be abstract, and likely consists of multiple overlapping groups, what the large group shares is an identification with the victims of oppression.

The claim, then, that neutrality always helps the oppressor is really a watchword that defines the group organized around identification with the oppressed. This group also conceives of the world as containing only two groups, the oppressors and the oppressed, such that no one is permitted to stand outside or in between.

The second striking aspect of this portion of Wiesel's speech is his exhortation to make every site of oppression or victimization a momentary "center of the universe." This notion, that places of violence, trauma, and persecution must become metaphorical centers of the universe, expresses a fantasy about change and victimization that will be elaborated immediately below.

For now, we may describe the fantasy as one in which the group's victimization becomes "central" to everyone else in the world. Here, the "gravity" of victims' suffering pulls together all that exists, incorporating all into a single moral universe where everything "revolves" around the victim's experience, beliefs, and fantasies. This change would indeed be "cosmic": It would privilege the victim and would demarcate the movements of both victims and victimizers, while casting to the outer reaches of space those least involved with victimization.

The fantasy suggested by Wiesel's speech is one in which victims stand at the center of a new moral "universe," pushing and pulling others along prescribed paths, moving and activating all those around them.

If we stay with this metaphor, the activity of the victims implied here is twofold: on one hand, the center *does not move* but remains stationary, while other objects revolve around it; on the other hand, to the extent that this center has mass, it gradually pulls in and, eventually, consumes everything in its gravitational field.

6.

The difference I am highlighting here is the difference between being the "center of the universe," on one hand, and being a "center of initiative" (Kohut 1977, 99), on the other. To be the latter is to be a creative and autonomous agent capable of initiating thought, action, and change in the world and, simultaneously, relating to others as separate subjects, external to the self. Placing victimization, persecution, or trauma at the center of a moral universe encourages persons and groups to become, in Cathy Caruth's words, centers or "site[s] of [shared] trauma" (1995, 11), rather than centers or sites of autonomous being, doing, and relating.

Due to limitations of space, it is impossible here to give a complete accounting of the process by which the valorization of suffering and trauma impedes real change (Bowker 2016). What may be said is that in idealization of victimhood and suffering we find a *fantasized* hypertrophy and monopolization of subjectivity, such that the victimized person or group envisions itself to be the only vital, active agent in the world.

This grandiose fantasy appears as a "reaction formation" against experiences or convictions of utter powerlessness. The concomitant denial of separateness, reality, and agency to others leaves the person or group in sole possession of the power to make change, and yet, as Wiesel's astronomical metaphor reminds us, the central object does not move or change but only induces movement and change in others.

While this fantasy of change offers a kind of hope, it is, in many respects, a deeply conservative fantasy, if we may so speak, for its primary objective is to secure the identification with the victim, rather than to act in ways that make meaningful differences for the self or others. Dedication to this fantasy serves not only to defend against the conviction that the self or group is powerless, but to distract from other threats to the identity of the person or group.

As some readers will know, there are many individuals, families, and organizations who are "addicted" to change of a certain kind: disruptive, chaotic, and superficial change (see, e.g., Kagan and Schlosberg 1989). Crisis, urgency, and turbulence serve, paradoxically, to stabilize such persons or groups: They remain, somehow, in "the center of the storm." In such cases, "change" both defines the identity of the person or group *and* distracts from awareness of threatening realities, the most threatening of which is the need for meaningful, substantive, internal change.

Such a situation, then—opposed, as it is, to much of the psychoanalytic enterprise—may be described not merely as "change for change's sake," but, more precisely, as change for the sake of *not* changing. As David Levine suggests in his extraordinary essay, we may understand a good deal of organizational change in terms of a manic state: "manic" in that it relies on a "fantasized identification between a primitive self and its ideal" (1999, 231), and "manic" in the more causal sense of urgent, frenzied, and compulsively-driven activity that defends against contact with what is real in the self, the organization, and the world.

7.

Camus once insisted that "he who has understood reality does not rebel against it, but rejoices in it; in other words, he becomes a conformist" (1956, 156). To be engaged in Camus's fantasy of change — to be a "rebel," which is Camus's more romantic term for today's "change agent" — then, requires a *misunderstanding* of reality that precludes real change.

When we refuse to understand reality, we refuse to understand the psychic meaning of "reality" as a place where others and events exist independently of ourselves. In such a world, there are no boundaries, and therefore, no possibility of relating, communicating, or thinking; only joining or opposing, conspiring or rebelling.

When the fantasy described above is operative, the language used to describe change — its nature, its necessity, its goal — is vague and grandiose, characterized by an urgency and a vigilance that borders on compulsiveness, and features reactive elements more prominently than active ones (i.e., a preoccupation with monitoring and reacting to stimuli that confirm the beliefs and assumptions of the group).

In some cases, the changes demanded are so extreme that they may be understood to be impossible by design. In this case, we can see how the conservative element in the fantasy directly opposes any truly "progressive" activity it purports to undertake: Making impossible demands or insisting upon impossible changes stymies efforts to create real change and, most likely, entrenches resistance and opposition to change. But, of course, failure to achieve change and success in provoking resistance, as discussed above, may well be the unconscious goals embedded in this sort of activity.

Admittedly, the fantasies and realities of change are not so easily distinguishable when faced with the challenges of daily life.

8.

Let us consider something smaller, and, perhaps, more personal.

Camus's early three-act play *Le malentendu* [*The Misunderstanding*] borrows thematic elements from classical tragedy, alludes explicitly to Gospel narrative, references structural and character elements from the Renaissance *commedia dell'arte,* and propels its action in ways reminiscent of situation comedies modernized by Shakespeare but perhaps most familiar to contemporary audiences via televised serials.

The plot of *The Misunderstanding* is rather simple: Jan is a wealthy, married, middle-aged man who, on hearing of his father's death, returns after twenty years of absence to the small Moravian inn where his mother and sister live and work.

Jan is not immediately recognized by his family, due, in part, to his extended absence and, in part, to his mother's and sister's habit of sparing attention to guests whom they intend to rob and murder. Jan also takes care to hide his identity from them, ostensibly in order to gather information about them, to gain "a better notion of what to do to make them happy" (Camus 1958, 84), and to set up a joyful surprise when he eventually reveals himself.

Jan's ruse is protested by his wife, Maria, who accompanies him but whom he sends away for his first night at the inn. Jan's mother and sister, Martha, mistaking him for a wealthy solitary traveler, murder him and dump his body in the river before his identity is revealed.

Upon realizing what she has done, his mother drowns herself in the river where she and Martha killed Jan. Martha, now alone and in despair, will hang herself. Maria in agonizing grief, pleads for help and mercy but is heard only by an aged, taciturn servant, who replies, simply: "No."

9.

Beyond associations with Camus's absurd philosophy, there are two main "moral" conclusions scholars have derived from the play. The first is that Jan's quest for recognition, for his identity to be seen and known by his family, is impossible and, thus, is destined to bring disaster.

Jan, on this account, suffers from a sort of Hegelian *hubris,* believing he can be recognized and that his family's recognition will bring him infinite happiness, erasing the pain of their long estrangement.

Certainly, such an interpretation seems to fit Camus's philosophical project, which asks us to recognize that our "sin[ful]" desire to know and our "wild longing for clarity" are unfulfillable, impossible, and destructive (1955, 21). To chase after understanding and recognition seems, in some of Camus's writing, to lead only to violence and death, whereas internalizing the inevitability of failure — as in our fundamental "absurdity" — permits us to survive (see Bowker 2014).

The second, and nearly opposite, interpretation is that the play proclaims the ethical necessity of open dialogue and communication, while condemning silence and obfuscation (see, e.g., Matherne 1971, 74–77; Willhoite 1968, 64–66). This conclusion was advanced by Camus, himself, after the play suffered a poor reception. Camus claimed it was

> a play of revolt, perhaps even containing a moral of sincerity. [...] If a man wants to be recognized, one need only tell him who he is. If he shuts up or lies, he will die alone, and everything around him is destined for misery. If, on the contrary, he speaks the truth, he will doubtless die, but after having helped himself and others to live. (quoted in Todd 2000, 186)

This extremely facile interpretation, although offered by the author himself, is confounding and perhaps backward, for recognizing a person surely means something other than "tell[ing]" that person "who he is." In the best of cases, this interpretation would flatten an already bare drama, making *The Misunderstanding* the simplest of cautionary tales.

Indeed, such an interpretation closely resembles the simplistic conclusion reached by Meursault when Camus places a prototype of the story of *The Misunderstanding* in *L'étranger* [*The Stranger*]. Here, Meursault describes the idea of hiding one's identity from one's family as "a joke" (*plaisanterie*) (Camus 1988, 80). If "nothing distinguishes jokes or jests more from other psychological structures than their double-sidedness or duplicity" (Freud 1960, 213–14), then jokes must always conceal or confound their own expression, must "muddle" their true intentions (Camus 1958, 83), and, in this sense, must always miscommunicate and must always be misunderstood.

Of the story, Meursault concludes: "On the one hand it wasn't very likely. On the other, it was perfectly natural. Anyway, I thought the traveler pretty much deserved what he got and that you shouldn't play games" (Camus 1988, 80). While Meursault is not always the keenest observer of human emotion, he is right that Jan's gambit is like a joke and a game because it appears to be a species of play, play being a form of creative experimentation where impulses are heeded and where some departures from the rules of reality are tolerated, as in the dramatic medium called the *play*.

10.

It may seem callous to discuss a drama full of violence and tragedy in relation to jokes or games or play. But there is something to be learned in this comparison. First, it reminds us that Jan's actions express impulses and fantasies that may belong to the periods of life in which playing is of the greatest import: infancy and childhood.

Second, Jan does not play *well,* not only because the consequences of his playing are disastrous, but because he is unable to enact or realize his play in the space between his subjective imagination and his objective interactions with his mother and sister. This makes his playing frustrating and agonizing, to him and to Maria, who strenuously objects to his ruse on precisely these grounds, insisting that "there's something [...] something morbid about the way you're doing this" (Camus 1958, 83).

Contrary to the two "moral" conclusions cited above, the real tragedy of *The Misunderstanding* derives from Jan's unconscious desire to re-experience his family's misrecognition and neglect, a traumatic experience he suffered years ago, which he re-lives by undertaking an elaborate deception.

One clue about the unconscious motivations of Jan's actions comes when he describes his ruse as the inevitable result of his "dreams," by which he seems to mean both dreams experienced in sleep and hopes of a happy reunion with his family, upon which depends his ability to "find his true place in the world" (1958, 87).

Jan's dedication to his unlikely "dream" of resolving twenty years of estrangement and psychological suffering by orchestrating a surprise announcement of himself remains strong even as he begins to realize the potentially devastating outcomes of his actions.

This inflexible pursuit of his "dream," in spite of his family's clear inability to respond in the way he had hoped, also tells us something about Jan's unconscious motivations and, therefore, about one of the subtler *malentendus* in the play.

What really compels Jan to play this trick on his family? Why does he not heed his wife's advice to announce himself immediately? Maria oversimplifies things, but is not entirely wrong in suggesting that, "on such occasions one says, 'It's I,' and then it's all plain sailing."

It is "common sense," she argues, that "if one wants to be recognized, one starts by telling one's name. [...] Otherwise, by pretending to be what one is not, one simply muddles everything" (Camus 1958, 83).

It would seem sensible for Jan to introduce himself, as Maria instructs him, to say: "I'm your son. This is my wife. I've been living with her in a country we both love, a land of endless sunshine beside the sea. But something was lacking there to complete my happiness, and now I feel I need you" (84). But, of course, for Jan, and for Camus, and likely for many others, relating to one's family is not "so simple as all that" (84).

Jan tells Maria that one of his aims in concealing his identity is to "take this opportunity of seeing [his mother and sister] from the outside" (83), to become informed about how to make his family happy. But it is not clear why Jan should expect his family to be more revealing or honest when standing before a stranger than before a son. Furthermore, to see others "from the outside" by making them naïve about one's identity risks exposing them to embarrassment, registered by a hidden "eye" (a hidden "I") of which they are unaware.

Jan's aim to hide, then reveal, his identity is a type of deception that manipulates the emotions of his family, and perhaps his own emotions as well. Jan has made the family naïve about an important piece of information. To make someone naïve, as in practical jokes, may lead the naïve person to speak or act in a way that is inappropriate, humiliating, or shocking to those privy to the withheld information. The "practical joke," as it were, is "on" the naïve person because she is not "in" on the joke. The victim of such a joke is "unmasked" when she who once loomed large is revealed to be flawed or ridiculous. As in satire, a portion of the pleasure of joking lies in depicting those who are exalted (*erhaben*) as vulgar or stupid (Freud 1960, 248).

For Freud, in joking, in satire, and in deceptions, we experiment with aggressive impulses, in which we discover a way to inflict suffering upon others without excessive guilt. More specifically, deceptions and jokes of this nature impose upon their victims experiences resembling the helplessness of childhood (Freud 1960, 280–84): The naïve subject of the joke is exposed in a moment of childlike confusion, ignorance, humiliation, or anxiety, particularly when provoked into losing control or unwittingly transgressing social or moral norms. This aggressive impulse to provoke, then witness, helplessness in others likely arises in connection with the instigator's own experiences of helplessness, although such experiences are not always consciously recalled. In this way, such deceptions may actually be attempts to *transmit* painful or traumatic experiences onto others via projective identification, to re-experience them through others, and even to forge renewed connections with others based upon a suffering now shared.

It is important, in the context of *The Misunderstanding,* to ask how Jan's family members could be expected to feel after having been seen "from the outside" treating their own son and brother as a perfect stranger, selling him beer and making up his room. Although Jan's mother is devastated at having taken part in his murder, it is not precisely her killing of Jan that she laments most profoundly. Rather, she is deeply aggrieved by her mistaking of Jan. "When a mother is no longer capable of recognizing her own son," she claims, "it's clear that her role on earth is ended" (Camus 1958, 120). Even had Jan not been murdered, it is certain that his ruse would have succeeded in making his mother's misrecognition of him all too clear. It seems likely, therefore, that Jan's aim is not to happily surprise his family by exposing his identity, but to expose his family's failure to recognize him. Of course, Jan succeeds in exposing this failure, and thereby re-experiences the earlier traumatic instance of this failure, all too well.

II.

Jan's first line of defense against the idea of openly communicating is to suggest that he has played no part in the deception. When he is "given a glass of beer, against payment," "received [...] without a word," and "looked at, but [not] *seen*" (Camus, 1958, 82–83, emphasis in original), he claims to be stunned, deciding only at that moment to remain silent and "let things take their course."

Maria correctly objects, however, that there is no "thing" to take its course, that, instead, the "thing" to which Jan refers is actually "another of those ideas of yours." To this comment Jan retorts: "It wasn't an idea of mine, Maria; it was the force of things" (83).

Jan's denial of his part in fabricating the deception, a denial of his own free will, suggests that he is once again silenced by his family's treatment of him, that he finds himself paralyzed, perhaps re-experiencing the moment when his mother sent him off so coldly twenty years before. "My mother didn't come to kiss me," Jan recalls, tellingly. "At the time I thought I didn't care" (82). This withholding of affection, this non-existent farewell by Jan's mother, involves the rejection of him at a precarious moment of separation, at the very moment when he literally separated himself from his family.

Jan's mother's rejection of him at this moment expresses her rejection of him as a separate self, her refusal or inability to relate with him as someone other than a family member. This event, and what it likely reflects about a pattern of behavior in Jan's family, appear to have been to some degree traumatic for Jan, not only because of their lasting effects on his emotional life and his inability to be happy, but in the "latency" or delay (*Nachträglichkeit*) of their impacts: "At the time I thought I didn't care."

Jan does not *feel* that he has a choice. His deception appears to him to be necessary, just as he assigns responsibility for his choices to forces outside of himself. Imagining one's choices to be necessary consequences of forces outside of the self is one way to misunderstand oneself, to remain unaware of one's true intentions, and to pursue aims about which one remains unconscious.

Externalizing necessity and responsibility is also common in repetitive and ritualized behavior, particularly that associated with the compulsive element in traumatic repetition: the feeling that one is not in control, that one is "forced" to re-visit a traumatic scene either literally, in dreams, or in obsessive behaviors that express or reflect traumatic material.

12.

While little is offered by Camus on the subject of Jan's childhood, conversations between his mother and Martha suggest that in his family—as was likely the case in Camus's own family—one is either "in" or "out." Even when "in," of course, one is not recognized as a separate person but merely as a family member.

Incredibly, Jan's mother fully admits as much, saying she "might have forgotten her daughter [Martha], too," if Martha hadn't "kept beside me all these years [...] probably that's why I know she is my daughter" (95).

Martha is only known by her mother, only recognized, because she is literally beside her mother. She is only recognized as a mother's daughter, not as an individual.

The mother's rejection of Jan at the moment of his physical departure therefore seems to reflect a dilemma of relating that predated it, a dilemma in which relatedness with family members across difference or distance was impossible. Faced with such a dilemma, Jan would have had to choose between being absolutely exiled and, in some sense, "dead" to his family, and being permanently "beside" his family only to receive acknowledgment as a family member.

In other words, in such a family as Jan's, there is no relatedness. Instead, there is a schizoid *either/or,* whereby one either exists in an immersive co-presence with the family, or, if one attempts separation in any of its forms, one does not exist at all. Once Jan decides to leave his family, he ceases to exist. Thus, for his mother, there was, in some sense, *no one there* to kiss farewell.

Children raised in conditions similar to these are forced to make a terrible choice at a young age: to identify with a parent's or the family's needs and to serve those needs as a family member, or to face emotional exile by heeding the child's need to explore and discover something authentic and unique within himself (see, e.g., Miller 1997; Winnicott 1965).

Of course, since the child is both physically and emotionally dependent upon the parent and the family, the choice is really no choice at all, as such children must almost instinctively learn to repress not only their needs but their awareness of them, for any outbursts of emotion reflective of their discomfort — for instance, rage at those who demand self-negation, or grief at the loss of self-expression — would only provoke retaliation from the family in the form of further neglect, deprivation, or abandonment.

These dynamics are readily apparent throughout the play, particularly when Jan speaks about his sense of "duty" toward his family (Camus 1958, 84–85), a rather mysterious duty, presumably neglected for twenty years, by which he must now make a conscious effort to procure the family's "happ[iness]" (84), while at the same time refusing to announce his true identity, and while misrecognizing and repressing his own needs in relation to his family. "I don't need them," he insists, "but I realized they may need me" (84).

13.

Jan does admit a desire to "find his true place in the world" (87), and the play asks us to imagine that he strives to establish this place by returning to his family and "making happy those I love. [...] I don't look any farther" (87). But, of course, Jan's act of concealing his identity succeeds neither in making his family happy nor in bringing him closer to finding his "true place." The "true place" Jan seeks is really a regressive experience, an experience meant to substitute for a genuine "place" for himself amidst his family, which he knows to be impossible.

This regressive experience Jan seeks is, in many ways, *the opposite* of finding a home or a "place," for he unconsciously desires not to be recognized but to be misrecognized, not to be welcomed but to be rebuffed, not to find joy and reunion but to re-encounter his rage and grief at his unfeeling expulsion from the family.

To understand these claims, we must recall that although Jan has clearly designed his charade in advance, telling Maria that her unexpected presence at the hotel "will upset all [his] plans" (82), when he enters the inn, he says that he "expected a welcome like the prodigal son's" (83).

Why, we may wonder, would Jan consider playing his trick if he sincerely expected such a joyous reception? Since this is not the sole reference to the story of the prodigal son in the Book of Luke — later, Jan raises the cup of poisoned tea to his lips and calls it "the feast of the returning prodigal" (109) — and since that story is, itself, full of ambivalence, misrecognition, and resentment between members of a family, it is worth a moment to analyze this reference.

In Luke, the prodigal son, having wasted his inheritance "with riotous living," now in fear of starvation, returns to his father, saying: "I have sinned against heaven, and in thy sight, and am no more worthy to be called thy son" (15:21, KJV). The ashamed son plans to offer himself as a servant to his father's household, as he feels assured that he no longer deserves recognition even as a member of the family (15:19).

But the prodigal son's father rejoices that "this my son was dead, and is alive again" (15:24), giving him fine robes and preparing a lavish feast in his honor. Such treatment arouses jealous rage in the elder brother, who complains that, while he has toiled and served beside his father his whole life, he has never been given such gifts nor inspired comparable joy in his father. In reply, the father attempts to reassure the elder son of his indelible membership in the family: "Son, thou art ever with me, and all that I have is thine" (15:31).

Jan's reference to this story and his self-identification as the prodigal son, then, suggest several things about his feelings and intentions regarding his family. Although he has not wasted his family's fortune on debauchery, he feels ashamed. He is likely aware of the possibility of a negative or unsatisfying reception. He may fear, in particular, the reaction of his sister Martha, who has remained by her mother's side and, in so doing, has not enjoyed the same freedom, travel, romance, or fortune as he has. He may feel or anticipate guilt at the contrast between his seemingly separate existence and his sister's lifelong enmeshment with their mother and their home.

Jan's mother's treatment of Martha is similar to that of the father toward the elder son in the story of the prodigal: The father's reply to the elder son does not directly address the elder's son's complaint that he has never been "recognized" as special or worth celebrating. Instead, the father offers an erasure of boundaries between the son, the father, and all that belongs to the family: The elder son's unique self is still overlooked, while, in returning from "the dead," the prodigal son seems to have found a form of loving recognition.

Like the prodigal son, Jan fears announcing himself and incurring the rejection of his family because he has at least partly internalized his family's insistence that his separateness is tantamount to his being "dead." While the prodigal son in Luke feared his own literal death by starvation, if Jan has internalized the equation of separateness with death, then Jan may feel psychically "dead" while separated from his family. Unlike the prodigal son however, Jan cannot bring himself to announce that he has returned. He cannot make himself "alive again."

Jan says he expected a welcome like the prodigal son's, but his ruse assures that he will receive exactly what the prodigal son feared: an experience of indifference from the family and treatment as an outsider.

Indeed, after Jan's mother admits she "might have forgotten her daughter" had she left her side, she adds, "if a son came here, he'd find exactly what an ordinary guest can count on: amiable indifference, no more and no less" (Camus 1958, 96).

Just as the prodigal son imagines that he may be forced to take on the identity of a servant to the family, rather than being a member of the family, Jan assumes a second identity when he pretends to be a mere lodger. Both a servant and a lodger can be expected to elicit, if not indifference, something far less than familial intimacy. As in the prodigal son's offer to make himself a servant in penance for his sins, Jan seems to heap emotional punishment upon himself by pretending to be a mere stranger.

14.

According to Jan, his desire to return home is derived from the fact that, in his separation from the family, he and his family have been lost or dead to each other. He desires to revive his connection, however, with a family that offers only self-occluding family membership or nothing. While he pretends to seek recognition from and a mature relationship with his family, he must be at least partly aware that his family is incapable of recognizing and relating with him as a separate self.

Thus, if he does seek to revive a relationship with his family, it can only be one based on immediate presence, family membership, and de-subjectified reunion. In this light, it is a matter of some importance that Maria offers him a more profound and more complete loving recognition of his self. "I've always loved everything about you, even what I didn't understand, and I know that really I wouldn't wish you to be other than who you are" (85). Tragically, Jan forsakes this apparently mature, loving relationship to re-enact a drama of silence, loss, and death with his family.

To summarize:

Jan's odd yet carefully crafted deception permits him to re-experience something of his original rage and grief while inflicting pain and humiliation upon his family.

At the same time, he protects himself from the possibility of further trauma and protects his family from his resentment and anger.

He pursues his deception in a way that leaves his family a way out, an absolution from responsibility for this instance of misrecognition, since it is, after all, his deception and not their hateful indifference that misleads them *this* time.

His ruse, therefore, partly protects his mother and sister, which expresses an underlying identification with his family, with those who abandoned him, rather than with his self, which felt and which continues to feel abandoned.

Indeed, it is fair to say that Jan, rather than being able to make himself "alive again" before his family, has made himself a stranger to them, which suggests that his action may also express his desire to take responsibility for the loss associated with separation.

Jan's deception allows him to hold on to his conscious estimations of his feelings and intentions — that he is happy, that he does not "need" his family, and that he wishes to make his family happy — along with his unrealistic hope for a loving reception by his family.

It permits him to safely recall an otherwise dangerous and anxiety-provoking rage and grief while "muddling" those feelings with the pretenses of his ruse.

It permits him to internalize responsibility for his family's rejection of him while protecting his family from the punchline of his joke, as it were.

Perhaps most importantly, it succeeds in replaying *the very experience* that he both dreads and needs, the experience that set him apart from his family for twenty years, the experience of standing before his family as a separate person and being unrecognized, unseen, unknown.

By repeating this traumatic experience, Jan finds a way to identify with his family and their extreme demand that one either belong or die, that one be in or out.

Jan, therefore, seems to seek, and to find, not loving recognition for himself, but only a "morbid" repetition of a traumatic experience from his past.

Missing Persons

1.

Persons go missing all the time.
A thousand abdications for every abduction.
I am not making light of—

2.

In "Obóz głodowy pod Jasłem" ["Jaslo Hunger Camp"],
Wisława Szymborska writes:
"History rounds off skeletons to zero.
A thousand and one is still only a thousand.
That *one* seems never to have existed" (1997, 42).

3.

But by the time we're counting skeletons—
To be accounted among the dead is not—
To be the thousand and first skeleton—
To lament a missing one among a missing multitude—
Persons do not come to matter in this way.

4.

Whether a person has existed—
Whether a person has been—
It is not a question for history.

A Dream of Not Recovering from a Drug

I've unwittingly swallowed an extraordinarily potent and unfamiliar hallucinogenic drug.

Once ingested, I am told this drug will never leave my body.

I will never be rid of it. It will never be rid of me.

I could, theoretically, seek help, but the drug makes this impossible.

I keep forgetting what is real.

I keep forgetting whether I am having fun or in a panic state.

I am alone but amidst others.

I can speak and laugh with them, but I cannot communicate or expel—which, at times, feel as if they were the same thing—what is inside me.

I am unable to carry out the simplest of plans, such as walking across a room, without suddenly realizing that I am already falling through a yawning, elastic hole in the middle of the floor.

I will never recover.

I will remain in a state of incomprehensible madness for the rest of my life.

I may die.

Even if I live, I will not recognize myself.

Before I wake, I recall that in spite of my horror, this dream, like all dreams, comprises equal parts: dread and wish.

References

Alford, C.F. 2009. *After the Holocaust: The Book of Job, Primo Levi, and the Path to Affliction.* New York: Cambridge University Press.

Barthes, R. 1971. *Mythologies.* Translated by A. Lavers. Paris: Farrar, Strauss & Giroux.

Beckett, S. 1956. *Waiting for Godot: A Tragicomedy in Two Acts.* New York: Grove Weidenfeld.

Bentham, J. 1791. *Panopticon, or the Inspection-House.* Dublin and London: T. Payne.

Berlant, L., and L. Edelman. 2013. *Sex, or the Unbearable.* Durham: Duke University Press.

Berlyne, D.E. 1949. "'Interest' as a Psychological Concept." *British Journal of Psychology* 39, no.4: 184–95. DOI: 10.1111/j.2044-8295.1949.tb00219.x.

Bernardin de Saint-Pierre, J.H. 1895. *Paul et Virginie, suivi de la chaumière indienne.* Paris: Garnier.

Bion, W.R. 1982. *The Long Week-End, 1897–1919: Part of a Life.* Abington: Fleetwood Press.

———. 2001. *Experiences in Groups and Other Papers.* East Sussex: Brunner-Routledge.

Block, S.M. 2011. "The Plano Suicides." *Granta* 118. https://granta.com/the-plano-suicides.

Boudry, M. 2014. "The Art of Darkness." *Scientia Salon,* July 7. https://scientiasalon.wordpress.com/2014/07/07/the-art-of-darkness.

Bowker, M.H. 2014. *Rethinking the Politics of Absurdity: Albert Camus, Postmodernity, and the Survival of Innocence.* New York and London: Routledge.

———. 2016. *Ideologies of Experience: Trauma, Failure, Deprivation, and the Abandonment of the Self.* New York and London: Routledge.

Camus, A. 1948. *The Plague.* Translated by S. Gilbert. New York: Vintage.

———. 1955. *The Myth of Sisyphus and Other Essays.* Translated by J. O'Brien. New York: Vintage.

———. 1956. *The Rebel: An Essay on Man in Revolt.* Translated by A. Bower. New York: Vintage.

———. 1958. *The Misunderstanding.* In *Caligula and Three Other Plays,* translated by S. Gilbert, 75–134. New York: Vintage.

———. 1988. *The Stranger.* Translated by M. Ward. New York: Vintage.

Caruth, C., Ed. 1995. *Trauma: Explorations in Memory.* Baltimore: Johns Hopkins University Press.

Csikszentmihalyi, M. 1990. *Flow: The Psychology of Optimal Experience.* New York: Harper & Row.

De Conihout, I. 2016. "The Most Notorious Gun in French Literature." *Christie's,* November 23. https://www.christies.com/features/The-gun-Paul-Verlaine-used-to-shoot-Arthur-Rimbaud-comes-to-auction-7950-3.aspx.

Dewey, J. 1913. *Interest and Effort in Education.* Boston: Houghton Mifflin.

Durington, M. 2008. "The Ethnographic Semiotics of a Suburban Moral Panic: Teenagers, Heroin and Media in Plano, Texas." *Critical Arts* 21, no. 2: 261–75. DOI: 10.1080/02560040701810040.

Foucault, M. 2000. "On the Genealogy of Ethics: An Overview of a Work in Progress." In *Ethics: Subjectivity and Truth —*

Essential Works of Foucault, 1954–1984, Vol. 1, edited by P. Rabinow, translated by R. Hurley, 253–80. London: Penguin.
Freud, S. 1959. *Group Psychology and the Analysis of the Ego.* Translated by J. Strachey. New York: W.W. Norton.
———. 1960. *Jokes and Their Relation to the Unconscious.* Translated by J. Strachey. New York: W.W. Norton.
Grotstein, J.S. 2007. *A Beam of Intense Darkness: Wilfred Bion's Legacy to Psychoanalysis.* London: Karnac Books.
Guntrip, H. 1992. *Schizoid Phenomena, Object Relations and the Self.* Madison: International Universities Press.
James, W. 1950. *The Principles of Psychology*, Vol. 1. New York: Dover.
Kafka, F. 1971. *Kafka: The Complete Stories and Parables.* Edited by Glazer. Translated by W. Muir and E. Muir. Berlin: Schocken Books.
Kagan, R., and Schlosberg, S. 1989. *Families in Perpetual Crisis.* New York and London: W.W. Norton.
Kierkegaard, S. 1946. "Either/Or." In *A Kierkegaard Anthology*, edited by R. Bretall, translated by H.A. Johnson, 21–108. Princeton: Princeton University Press.
Kohut, H. 1977. *The Restoration of the Self.* Chicago: University of Chicago Press.
Lacan, J. 1970. *Le séminaire. Livre XVII. L'envers de la psychanalyse, 1969–70.* Edited by J.-A. Miller. Paris: Éditions de Seuil.
———. 1975. *Le séminaire. Livre XX. Encore, 1972–73.* Edited by J.-A. Miller. Paris: Éditions de Seuil.
———. 1998. *The Seminar of Jacques Lacan: On Feminine Sexuality, the Limits of Love and Knowledge (Encore) (Book XX).* Edited by J.-A. Miller and B. Fink. Translated by B. Fink. New York: W.W. Norton.
Levine, D.P. 1999. "Creativity and Change: On the Psychodynamics of Modernity." *American Behavioral Scientist* 43, no. 2: 225–44. DOI: 10.1177/00027649921955236.
Limbaugh, R. 2012a. "Why Mr. Roads and Bridges Hates Suburbia." *The Rush Limbaugh Show,* October 3. http://www.rushlimbaugh.com/daily/2012/10/03/why_mr_roads_and_bridges_hates_suburbia.

———. 2012b. “Obama’s Plan to Eliminate Suburbs.” *The Rush Limbaugh Show,* August 8. https://www.rushlimbaugh.com/daily/2012/08/02/obama_s_plan_to_eliminate_suburbs.

Madsen, B.G. 1954. “Realism, Irony, and Compassion in Flaubert’s ‘Un cœur simple.’” *French Review* 27, no. 4: 253–58. https://www.jstor.org/stable/382914.

Matherne, B. 1971. “Hope in Camus’ ‘The Misunderstanding.’” *Western Speech* 35, no. 2: 74–87. DOI: 10.1080/10570317109373684.

Miller, A. 1997. *The Drama of the Gifted Child: The Search for the True Self.* Revised Edition. Translated by R. Ward. New York: Basic Books.

Moore, M. 1994. “Poetry.” In *The Complete Poems of Marianne Moore,* 36. New York: Penguin.

Plato. 1987. *The Republic.* 2nd Revised Edition. Translated by D. Lee. London: Penguin Books.

Reilly, K. 2016. “Read Elie Wiesel’s Nobel Peace Prize Acceptance Speech.” *Time.* July 2. http://time.com/4392267/elie-wiesel-dead-nobel-peace-prize-speech.

Rimbaud, A. 1886. *Les illuminations.* Paris: Publications de La Vogue.

———. 2000. *Rimbaud: The Works: A Season in Hell; Poems and Prose; Illuminations.* Translated by D.J. Carlile. Bloomington: XLibris.

Shawn, W. 2009. *Essays.* New York: Haymarket Books.

Showalter, E., Jr. 1966. “*Un Cœur simple* as an Ironic Reply to Bernardin de Saint-Pierre.” *French Review* 40, no. 1: 47–55. https://www.jstor.org/stable/385004.

Sontag, S. 1975. “Fascinating Fascism.” *New York Review of Books,* February 6. http://www.nybooks.com/articles/1975/02/06/fascinating-fascism.

Stevens, W. 1990. *The Collected Poems of Wallace Stevens.* New York: Random House.

Stiteler, R. 1983. “Why Plano? When Young People Choose to Die.” *D Magazine,* December. https://www.dmagazine.com/publications/d-magazine/1983/december/why-plano.

Stoppard, T. 1968. *Rosencrantz and Guildenstern Are Dead.* New York: Grove Press.

Szymborska, W. 1997. *Poems: New and Collected.* Translated by S. Baranczak and C. Cavanagh. New York: W.W. Norton.

Todd, O. 2000. *Albert Camus: A Life.* Translated by B. Ivry. New York: Carroll & Graf.

Verlaine, P. 1884. *Les poètes maudits.* Paris: Vanier.

Watkins, C. 2000. *American Heritage Dictionary of Indo-European Roots.* 2nd Edition. Boston: Houghton Mifflin Harcourt.

Willhoite, F. 1968. *Beyond Nihilism: Albert Camus's Contribution to Political Thought.* Baton Rouge: Louisiana State University Press.

Williams, E. 2007. "Of Cinema, Food, and Desire: Franz Kafka's 'Investigations of a Dog.'" *College Literature* 34, no. 4: 92–124. https://www.jstor.org/stable/25115460.

Winnicott, D.W. 1965. *The Maturational Processes and the Facilitating Environment: Studies in the Theory of Emotional Development.* Edited by M. Khan. London: Hogarth & The Institute of Psycho-Analysis.

———. 1986. *Home Is Where We Start From: Essays by a Psychoanalyst.* New York: W.W. Norton.

———. 1992. *Through Paediatrics to Psycho-Analysis: Collected Papers.* Edited by M. Khan. East Sussex: Brunner-Routledge.

Zupančič, A. 2017. *What Is Sex?* Cambridge: Massachusetts Institute of Technology Press.

"W. dreams, like Phaedrus, of an army of thinker-friends, thinker-lovers. He dreams of a thought-army, a thought-pack, which would storm the philosophical Houses of Parliament. He dreams of Tartars from the philosophical steppes, of thought-barbarians, thought-outsiders. What distance would shine in their eyes!"

— Lars Iyer

Made in the USA
Middletown, DE
02 July 2019